A

MAN'S BOOK
OF THE
SPIRIT

Daily Meditations for a Mindful Life

A
MAN'S BOOK
OF THE
SPIRIT

Daily Meditations for a Mindful Life

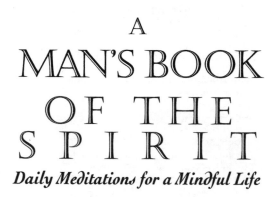

BILL ALEXANDER

AVON BOOKS  NEW YORK

A MAN'S BOOK OF THE SPIRIT: DAILY MEDITATIONS FOR A MINDFUL LIFE is an original publication of Avon Books. This work has never before appeared in book form.

AVON BOOKS
A division of
The Hearst Corporation
1350 Avenue of the Americas
New York, New York 10019

Copyright © 1994 by William M. Alexander, Jr.
Published by arrangement with the author
Library of Congress Catalog Card Number: 93-33892
ISBN: 0-380-77175-6

Library of Congress Cataloging in Publication Data:
Alexander, Bill.
    A man's book of the spirit : daily meditations for a mindful life / Bill Alexander.
        p.   cm.
    1. Men—Prayer-books and devotions—English. 2. Devotional calendars.   I. Title.
BL625.65.A54   1994   93-33892
291.4'3—dc20   CIP

First Avon Books Trade Printing: May 1994

AVON TRADEMARK REG. U.S. PAT. OFF. AND IN OTHER COUNTRIES, MARCA REGISTRADA, HECHO EN U.S.A.

Printed in the U.S.A.

OPM   10   9   8   7   6   5   4   3   2   1

To Kamala, Gia, David, Edward,
John, Elizabeth, and Willie
for their wild spirits
and their teachings
and
To Pauline Cerf Alexander

Introduction
and Acknowledgments

There is no men's movement.

A masculine awakening has been going on for over 20 years, more propelled by wild forces than led by charismatic individuals. This awakening has taken nearly as many forms as the number of men, and women, involved. Men have banded together: some to go into the woods with drums, some to study myth and fairy tales in order to recreate their own lives, others to reform divorce and custody laws, or to create new and innovative communities. Some formed groups in homes or churches to support each other in the process of waking up, of ending the enchantment. Many others began the process of change alone and only now are seeking support. We all began to awaken when the reality of an infantilized, utilitarian masculinity, molded to serve hard and narrow ends, had become too great to ignore and when the convenient palliatives, generally some form of the addictions to comfort or power, had failed.

This book assumes that at the heart of our pain was a spiritual crisis: The pain was from the loss of imagination and meaning. It was the pain of the dispirited man, fodder for wars, on others' soil or in corporatized economies. We were in pain from lack of ritual, lack of communion, and lack of connection—religious dilemmas all.

This pain was the beginning of the awakening of the spirited man. Reconnecting to our lives and our souls requires constant reaffirmation of the desire to do so; otherwise we have the experience only of a spiritual one-night stand. The awakening begins, but fades beneath the weight of the same ugly forces that hypnotized us in the first place.

A spiritual awakening is followed by spiritual practice and spirited action, loving attention to the tasks at hand, tasks that are not defined by narrow self-interest.

Here is how this book can work for you. Most days contain a quote, a reflection, and a prayer, exhortation or affirmation. Some are silly, some, I hope, are irritating. On some pages, you will find a task. These are intended to provide specific reconnection to our stories and to our communities. There are also "Mindful Days" throughout. These are days for men to connect more deeply with the stuff of everyday life, days of close attention to the gifts of the present moment. There are only eighteen such days in the book, but I encourage you to carry these practices into every day. The Appendix gives more details.

We are waking up and we are being unruly in the process. I believe the time has come to get in out of the woods, forgive whoever needs to be forgiven (and quickly), and take a look around at what needs to be done on the planet, in our homes, and in our souls, and then get to work, loving, spirit-centered, rowdy, and fiercely determined.

Thanks to Bob Mecoy, Editor-in-Chief at Avon Books, for the idea for this book and his support as I tried to figure out how to do it. Thanks also to Michail Reid for shepherding it along and for the title.

I am grateful to my brother Philip Alexander for years of endurance and caring, to dharma brother Hugh

O'Haire and spirit brothers Lenny Holzer and Mark Gero for their stories and heartfeltness.

James Park Morton, godfather to Willie Alexander, teacher and dear friend, thanks to you and to Pam for your hospitality and your embraces.

Leslie Breed—Agent, matchmaker, canyon-hiker and angel; thank you.

Years ago I met rogue philosopher and fellow Tennesseean Sam Keen at a "word-tasting" party in San Francisco. (Sam brought "sanguine." I had "propinquity"). Our friendship has enriched me from that moment. Thanks, Sam, for being always just a short step ahead.

Finally, I bow to the ancestors and, most humbly, Bill Alexander of McKenzie, Tennessee, and Nell McLeod Alexander of Brooksville, Mississippi, in gratitude for their passion, which fired my own.

A

MAN'S BOOK

OF THE

S P I R I T

Daily Meditations for a Mindful Life

January 1

This is a month of celebration of the dark, the creative, and a time of preparation for the healing and blooming of the earth in springtime to come. In this season of darkness, the earth draws closest to the sun, with earth Perihelion on the fourth. Makara Sankranti, the Indian festival of the passing of the winter solstice is celebrated as are Tu B'shivat, the Jewish celebration of the Trees, and Plow Monday, the blessing of tools in preparation for spring planting, on the first Monday after Epiphany.

This is a month to be reminded of "the fruitful darkness," the birth of nourishment through scarcity, and compassion through suffering.

The dark reveals the light.

January 2

We shall not cease from exploration
And the end of all our exploring
Will be to arrive where we started
And know the place for the first time.
—T.S. Eliot

In winter we can become aware of the movements of the earth, of the renewal of life and the beginnings of journeys upward. Paying attention, we can free ourselves of the clinging hoarfrost and move, with all creation, toward the light. We are beginning to awaken to an inevitable journey and our choices are to make that journey consciously or to stumble half-asleep, doomed by our stuckness only partially to unfold before the distant sun and cold winds of the late months force us downward again.

Turn over a rock and look for the pale white shoot forcing upward again. It will always journey toward the sun and it will always return to the earth. Unnourished, it returns little nourishment to the earth. Filled with sun and rain, it grows and bursts its bounds and brings home a full measure.

NOT FOR ONE DAY, NOT IN ONE LIFETIME, CAN I EXPECT TO NOURISH OTHERS IF I HAVE STARVED MYSELF.

January 3

Men weren't really the enemy—they were fellow victims suffering from an outmoded masculine mystique that made them feel unnecessarily inadequate when there were no bears to kill.
—BETTY FRIEDAN

The diversion of male bashing is both destructive and inevitable. It is true as well that some of the most virulent of the male bashers are male—a TV producer gives as the guiding spirit of his wildly successful sit-com the idea that "men are pigs." Sexual con-men denigrate the other guys and play at being "sensitive" in order to act out their own misogyny.

The spirited woman has a lot to teach her brothers. She has learned, through great effort, that we have created a false simplicity in the midst of vast complexity. She might say to us that there is no enemy other than ourselves, male and female, in a time of change and evolution. She might say that this change in our regard for each other will take time and effort. She might well ask for our ferocity, our protection, and our reason. In her nurturing and forgiving depths, she will seek forgiveness just as we seek to be forgiven for ignorance and fear. This forgiving is offered as the gift of one human blessing another. It is a gift of mutual healing.

THE VIGOROUS MAN SEEKS TO RECONCILE THE FATHER, THE WIFE, THE MOTHER, AND THE CHILD, NOT TO DEMONIZE THEM.

January 4

Outside the open window/
The morning air is all awash with angels.
—RICHARD WILBUR

Angels appear to us if we are watching. They appear in strange times and places and in the most ordinary moments. They are often not recognized at all. They might be prayed for, if we let our beliefs move that way, or might appear unbidden, unexpected, and even unnoticed. But they do appear and we have the choice of learning to see them. All of us have heard stories of strangers, never seen again, who performed feats of great strength or who pointed the way out of the darkest places, or spoke the surprising word in an innocent conversation; the word that lifted the fog of our fear and confusion. The word that revealed the presence of God for that moment. Many also have had the experience of a newcomer in his life leading him in new and terrifying directions, gently supporting and encouraging him.

It is difficult for men to say that these are angels. We have to cross too many lines that were laid down for many years. But seeing them can also show us a world of wonder that we knew as little boys, and can open our lives again to the sense of awe, gratitude, and joy that has been lost for too long to the grown man.

TODAY I WILL OPEN MY HEART TO THE PRESENCE
OF ANGELS IN MY LIFE.
WHO ARE THEY?

January 5

God is in the details.
—(attributed to LUDWIG MIËS VAN DER ROHE*)*

John Coltrane said that God breathes in us so gently and so completely that we scarcely know he is there. In our awakenings as men, we can begin to know that breath that breathes us. Some men find teachers, some meditate, some set aside a daily time for prayer and some talk with other men about the awakening of God. There is a great yearning in many of us now to know God, however we may search, whatever name we speak, whatever gender we feel her to be. It can be a great risk and an awe/full battle to reclaim him as our own. The cynical big brother scoffs at this struggle and rustles his balls, while the mother paints pictures of an effeminate child too fragile to bear a cross, and the teacher demands obedience to a supernatural old man. We felt this confusion years ago and if we could not reconcile it we buried it and it is screaming for our attention again. Now, as men, we can turn our backs to the old voices and see God coming from some other direction altogether.

I CAN ASK SOMEONE I TRUST ABOUT GOD. INCLUDING MYSELF.

January 6

> *Invest in the millennium. Plant sequoias.*
> *Say that your main crop is the forest*
> *That you did not plant,*
> *That you will not live to harvest.*
> —WENDELL BERRY
> *"Manifesto: The Mad Farmer*
> *Liberation Front"*

There are voices out there that are trying to get our attention if we could slow down long enough to listen for them. These are the voices of the forests, the woodlands, the dying topsoil, and the great swelling oceans, polluted by our greed and our speed. We have been destroying our Great Mother, all reverence gone.

Some other voices are calling us as well. The voices of loving men and women and the voices of our children are calling on us to put down our weapons and husband the earth. We can embrace the earth, our mother, and not plague her with our wars, great flaming pyres of oil, and earth sterilized until the millennium by "clean" bombs. We can hear that voice, frightened and timid, that speaks in our hearts and says "please stop," if we will just be still and practice great humility. We can make men's work the work of centuries to come rather than the work of the moment.

I CAN LEARN TO PRACTICE HUMILITY, PATIENCE, AND STILLNESS.
I CAN PRACTICE THE ETERNAL.

January 7

Mindful of the toxins I unconsciously choose every day, I will open myself to the silence and discover the sounds of life.

January 8

We need translators, bearing in mind that to translate without betrayal one must have experienced oneself the content that is to be carried across.
—ANANDA COOMARASWAMY

Advice to our brothers, our partners, and our children that is not born of direct experience is of no use. Men may absorb quantities of information, theory, and hot-sounding ideas from source after source. The TV shows us the "thirty minute" solution to every problem; books, like this one, are loaded with sound-bite smarts, and our fathers may have preached unexamined dogma, political, spiritual, or practical. But until we have leavened those grand ideas with our own gut-level experience, we are the equal only of the outside source. And our children, at least, are not fooled.

It is in heart speaking to heart that healing comes, slowly but with weight, power, and persistence. It is the offering of the gift of the self, physical, real, battered, and uplifted, that brings the transmission of wisdom.

🌳 🌳 🌳

I NEED TO LET MY EXPERIENCE CATCH UP WITH MY THOUGHTS.

January 9

And then to awake, and the farm, like a wanderer white
with the dew, come back, the cock on his shoulder: it was all
Shining, it was Adam and Maiden, the sky gathered again
and the sun grew round that very day.
—DYLAN THOMAS
"Fern Hill"

Awakening to beauty and renewal has become a manufactured event one morning out of thirteen on vacation. To feel the soul pounding in the chest when we experience some wonder again for the first time has become the province of the magazine editor or the tour guide. We have been taught how to avoid that beauty, by buying the manufactured thrills or by daily habits; reading the paper, drinking the coffee, drinking, smoking, eating, working, screwing, watching at public stages. We "earn" beauty and wonder by our tedium, rather than seeing it each day as part of our lives, entwined with every breath of our living. The sun rises each day. Each day and each night has its own rhythm, texture, odor, and sound. There is no good reason for any man to have to pay someone to allow him to "re-create." No manufactured event, paid for on the installment plan, can ever offer the scent of a child's hair, the feel of a lover's skin, the beauty of rain through trees in moonlight. Our awakening is an awakening of the senses as well as of the spirit.

I WILL TAKE THE TIME TO EMBRACE MY WORLD,
RIGHT HERE RIGHT NOW.

January 10

What homely bastards we are,
sitting here in the moonlight!
—BASHO
Translated by ROBERT AITKEN, *Roshi*

What a wonderful poem that is—loving one's homely old self and seeing the world around. It's a hard thing to laugh, quietly, at either our pretensions or their imperfections. Yet doing so is such a great relief that we can learn to do more.

We are bombarded with messages about how we should be. How we should be handsome, or successful money-makers, or great athletes, or studs. Not many fall into those ways, it seems. So many of us end up "homely"—sitting in the moonlight—pissed off. We wonder how it is that we ended up this unexpected way. "Why me?" we wonder. "Why not?" is the answer. We can strive to see that real self, to study it with a teacher or a friend or lover. We can learn to love it and nurture it and take it out into the moonlight. We can laugh, and feel shame slip away.

I CAN BE HONEST WITH MYSELF, ABOUT MYSELF, TO KNOW MYSELF.

January 11

It often seems like the voices are never going to let up. The voices saying "I just can't do this. I'm too . . ." fat, old, stupid, smart, sloppy, good, bad. These are the kind of messages that we chew up and digest into our nervous systems over the years until a kind of bland acceptance of inadequacy clouds our thoughts. Or perhaps we go right into denial and embrace our artifice, calling it "masculine"; that is, the way it's supposed to be.

We're not feeling that way anymore. Something is brewing. We may not be sure what it is that is on the way from those depths but it's not likely to go away. We are starting to see that the failure to study the whole self corrupts our lives. Robert Johnson says that every man must, in his life, and at the risk of his life for failing to do so, play every archetypal role.

I AM NOT TRAPPED IN MY LIFE. I CAN EXPAND TO FILL IT.

January 12

Mindful of the joy I felt as a child when unexpected good came my way, I will be playful and kind.

January 13

Hey!
What are you gawking at?
Don't you see, it's about you!
—SAWAKI ROSHI

A great master once said, "To study the way, is to study the self. To study the self is to forget the self." We sit right at the center of ourselves and rarely notice where we are. We have spent so much time making up stories about ourselves or building barriers to keep ourselves hidden, that the clearest view, that which is close at hand, is invisible. It is not acceptable to be a human "being." So when we begin to take a look at ourselves, if we are really persistent and trusting, we don't have an easy time of it at first. There comes quite a parade of faults and failings to haunt us. Many of us have always given up at this point. We have run away, saying "I am a man of action; I don't have time for this."

Now we are beginning to know that there is no time for anything else. If we are to be of service, we must begin to know the self. We are not alone any more. It is no longer "unmanly" to seek the spiritual way of life.

I'M NOT RUNNING FROM MYSELF ANYMORE.
I KNOW I MUST GO WITH ME.

January 14

Heaven calls you and revolves around you, showing you its timeless beauties, and your eye looks only at the earth.
—DANTE

Men must plod along, certainly, heavy with responsibility and burdened by the weight of ghosts. The earth is our home, after all, but the poet might be speaking of something other than that earth, which is only external. In the Lord's Prayer, we say "On earth as it is in heaven." Earth, in this case, might be that place of small concerns; a lesser place well worth tending, but a place in us that can be ennobled by the greater kingdom, the heavens, which we must reach with great effort. Just as many of us last looked in awe at the star-filled sky of early spring as children, so did we also last move in harmony with the greater pulse at that same young age.

Our memory of that wholeness with all that lives and moves, though neglected, is persistent and unchanged. We can awaken to our place, not apart but connected, not powerful but empowered. As we connect with the heaven surrounding us, our earth is transformed. As we look up, we are looking within.

AM I ABLE TO SENSE A GREATER PLACE FOR ME THAN I HAD YESTERDAY; AS GREAT AS THAT I KNEW AS A BOY? WHERE IS IT?

January 15

We cannot be happy if we expect to live all the time at the highest peak of intensity. Happiness is not a matter of intensity, but of balance and order and rhythm and harmony.
—THOMAS MERTON

In the past we have been awakened by radios set to rock and roll or the "news," which never seems new at all. We rushed through a process called getting-ready-to and then made sure we were entertained between bouts of working and feeding. We fell into bed exhausted and uncertain what had happened only to begin again after a night impoverished by lack of dreams and comfort. The scent of adrenalin is in the air.

Now we spend time not getting ready for anything, because so much is happening without our having to meddle with it.

WHAT'S HAPPENING TODAY?

January 16

Mindful of the pleasure of connection and distressed by the rush and anonymity of the crowd, I can encourage the risk of kindness.

January 17

Through Reverence for Life I raise my existence to its highest value and offer it to the world.
—ALBERT SCHWEITZER

Where have we hung our values? What have we "revered" as men? For decades, some say from the industrial revolution on, men have held as icons success, property, power, and money. All these have a place in the natural order of things, but the reverence debases us. This desire for things is not "wrong," it is painful. Our toys fail to amuse for long, and outlive us, gathering dust in dark closets in houses inhabited by toys and players but not by spirit. "Our banks grew taller than our temples."

As men are beginning to shift their values, to get a grasp on the eternal, to "Read not the Times, but the Eternities," a feeling of reverence for a power greater than ourselves is being born. The spirit awakes, uncertainly, but with great sparks of power and power to come, bringing hope as men revere life over senseless decay.

CAN I FIND MY WAY FROM THE PLAYPEN TO THE TEMPLE?

January 18

> *The irony of desire is that when you receive the object of desire, it creates that state of mind we call satisfaction for only a moment.*
> —STEPHEN LEVINE

I go from longing to satisfaction, and quickly to dissatisfaction as the object of my longing ceases to be that precise thing it was in my mind, before I attained it. "Look at my wonderful shiny motorcycle. I just got it" (object of satisfaction). "Is that dog pissing on my motorcycle?" (object of attachment and dissatisfaction). "Look at her wonderful shiny motorcycle" (new object of longing). This cycle will continue endlessly and the pain will not let up.

Men are beginning to see that desire, born in the mind, always disappoints. Men are beginning to experience that desire which erupts from the heart; "the desire to end desire" provides the only satisfaction.

🌿 🌿 🌿

WILL I EVER GET WHAT I WANT?

January 19

Easier said than does it.
—Anonymous

As we join with the struggle toward greater consciousness, toward a life of the spirit, it becomes easier to confuse the idea of the goal with its achievement. Talk of noble purposes loses its ring if we still yell at the children for being children, or snub our partners when they're feeling pain. And we are going to yell at the children and we're going to snub our partners and we are liable to spend a lot of time in action out of synch with our ideals. We can get caught in the nets of our own desires. Guilt at our imperfection at even this great purpose freezes us. The body becomes heavy and unmovable. The eyelids droop. The back of the throat becomes constricted and the ghost of a sob rises to the roof of the mouth. We're full of empty spiritual calories and it is time to stop consuming for a while.

AM I GETTING FAT?

January 20

Let us remember that sorrow alone is the creator of great things.
—ERNEST RENAN

For many years I could not bear to watch news stories about starving children in faraway lands. The sight of their deep eyes and hunger-deformed bodies repulsed me. The pain was too great. I turned my face away and hid in busywork. Yet each time I saw those images, I was shaken. Each time I saw them I felt repulsion and loathing.

Now I understand that pain as a summons to see what is really going on and as a demand for action.

Each of us in our day's walk is confronted with the faces of pain. As our lives move from this day onward, we can begin to acknowledge this pain as our own simply by refusing to look away. The images will be different for all of us. For some they will be close by, perhaps in our partner's hesitant caress. For others, they seem to be a great distance, glimpsed on so-called eyewitness news programs. They will appear for us all, just as they always have.

Our considerations of suffering are deeply sensitizing ones. For many men, conditioned by the expectations of women and the patriarchy, this is an awe-filled experience. Like Bartelby, we would prefer not to be inconvenienced. It is important to affirm for ourselves that the inevitable grief of a man's life enables him to relieve suffering.

❦ ❦ ❦

CONSIDER YOUR PAIN.

January 21

The whole earth is endowed with the same breath, rocks, trees, grass, earth, all animals, and men.
—HOPI *saying*
As recorded by ALEXANDER STEPHEN

We can embrace the earth, become sensually, intimately involved with it rather than seeing it as our background. Our fate as men is entwined, entangled, with the fate of every tree in sight. It is the same fate. Our treatment of this earth is our treatment of ourselves. The American Zen nun Myotai says "we had better see these trees as our fingernails."

Men have been misled. As boys some of us pitched our tents in fields where we didn't know the name of a single plant, fished in streams without knowing their source, threw rocks without noticing the trace of an ancient footprint preserved in curve.

As men, we can re-discover the warmth of soil, just below the surface, rich and crumbling. We can become intimate with the rough trees, the delicate grass. We can save ourselves as we save our home. We can husband the earth as we reclaim our spirits.

AM I ROOTED, OR ROOTLESS?

January 22

The road to wholeness is lined with sideshows and glittering attractions. Billboards advertise the circus just ahead with its promises of instant catharsis, and the laying of the queen's sword on the boy's shoulder to make him a man, and more, a hero. There are the bars, the whorehouses, the corporate offices, the videodromes, the superdomes, the "wildman" weekends all offering (distraction) fulfillment. How easily we are led to them, how warm the footstones and welcoming the barkers. We end up lost in the carny, disappointed, ashamed, and angry.

That, right there, is where the path can be found again, directly beneath your feet. The road to take, finally, is one's own. No one has walked that one before, but there are maps. The ancestors drew them and left them. They are in the libraries, sometimes, or they are on the streets. Your best friend might have them.

ASK.

January 23

A mindful day.

This is a day of mindfulness. What is sought here is not a unique day, standing distinctly apart from all others, but a day when the practice of mindfulness moves into the foreground. Today is a day of enrichment and heightened awareness. Please bring this wonderful practice into every day.

Mindfulness is not an esoteric practice. Being mindful simply means being awake. For men, being mindful can mean the beginning of the end of the social masculine trance and the dismembered life. In mindfulness we become aware of the fullness and flow of our lives, one moment at a time.

The Appendix of this book contains specific directions and suggestions. I encourage you to visit a library or bookstore for additional help in this ancient practice. One excellent book is *Full Catastrophe Living* by Jon Kabat-Zinn, Ph.D. The Vietnamese Buddhist monk Thich Naht Hahn has written dozens of books, many of which concern mindfulness. My personal favorites are *The Miracle of Mindfulness* and *Being Peace.*

This is a beautiful day. Please embrace it fully.

January 24

Mindful of the pleasure of slowing down and the rewards of change in daily habits, I will take some time in movement for myself.

WALK SLOWLY SOMEWHERE YOU NORMALLY GET TO
ANOTHER WAY!

January 25

The heart that breaks open can contain the whole universe.
—JOANNA NACY

We have discovered that the old ways, of material success, emotional frigidity, and hostile isolation were killing us off; our hearts were breaking and we called that heart attacks; our spirits were crumbling and we called that depression; our bodies were flaccid and cumbersome at thirty-five and we called that early middle age.

Then we discovered that there is no male midlife crisis but that men were in crisis, from the moment the doctor snipped off the end of their dicks to the moment they were pronounced dead, too soon, of something preventable, like war or success. We looked in the mirror and saw our fathers' faces or the faces of our most hated rivals. Rather than seeing ourselves as victims, we saw simply that our oppressor was dying and we were left alone and responsible to and for ourselves.

Then we felt another shift in our chests, our hearts opened to the love of God and our brothers and sisters whose absence for all those years had depleted our spirits so.

AT THE MOMENT OF GREATEST DESPAIR, WE BROKE THROUGH, NOT DOWN.

January 26

We come into this world alone, and alone we leave it;
and between the entrance and the exit,
we spend our time looking for companionship.
—E.M. DOOLING

We find soon enough that we must be engaged with others to survive, initially, then to grow and learn and prosper. Our first community is the family and, in our culture, this treasure is often wasted. The family has been lacerated by professional rowdies who claim crippling "dysfunction" in all families, but especially their own. The family has become the sentimental focus of shallow, mean-spirited politicians seeking scapegoats for their own profound inadequacies. And, indeed, many of us have come from sick, disheartened families, broken by fear, sustained by illusion.

Now we can look at where we are. Now. In our families we have the opportunity to enter into the richness of all roles and so to enrich ourselves. We are fathers, lovers, friends, and workers. But at times we may also be mothers, daughters, and sons. Our families enlarge us and bless us with a functioning greater than any we alone can find.

MY FAMILY IS MY GREATER BODY AND MIND.

January 27

If we don't know where we are, we don't know who we are.
—Wallace Stegner

Gary Snyder talks about the "radical act" of staying where we are and Wendell Berry speaks of being "placed." The wandering about, responsive to whim or to corporate fiat, spreads us too thin finally. Community and family give continuity, depth, and intimacy. Community demands that we sacrifice; family demands that we hold still.

You can't grow if you're not planted. We don't know where the water comes from that we drink, or the food that we eat. Our neighbors are strangers and the land nearby is a tourist attraction to be visited on weekends. We consider it a sign of achievement to live and work far above the ground, in towers taller than the churches and nearly reaching the heights of the bank buildings. Ungrounded, we become hungry and can't be filled. So we move. On the road again, the song says.

The road has to come to an end. As men shake off the tyranny of the patriarchy, we can come to value holding still, commitment, and community.

AM I READY TO HOLD STILL?

January 28

Hunger causes hunger.
—HUGH O'HAIRE

The Tibetans teach of a "hungry ghost"; a creature with a vast body and a tiny mouth. No matter how much it feeds, it can never be satisfied. No food can fill its endless belly, no drink will quench its thirst.

Many of us are in the peculiar position of having everything we need yet rather than being satisfied, we continue to consume. If we don't eat food, we eat clothes, or we eat cars, or gadgets, or forests and deserts. In our unquenchable thirst we drink our children's futures and we obliterate the subsistence of entire countries where the people, we pretend, are "other" than us.

Out of our fear, we eat the future without knowing it.

🌿 🌿 🌿

WHAT DO I PUT ON MY PLATE EACH DAY THAT IS NOT TRULY MINE?

January 29

Our own pulse beats in every stranger's throat.
—BARBARA DEMING

We need to begin to confront the lie of separation. Touching our lovers or playing with our children, each of us has the experience of connection. Dinner with friends can be a time of communion. As men who are awakening to the spiritual life, we are beginning to see that we are connected, intimately, with a greater community and that we are responsible to it and for it.

When we begin to know that we are a part of rather than apart from all our institutions we can begin the work of being peacemakers rather than warriors. Each man can find the power to say "I'm not going to do your killing this time." We can refuse to sacrifice our children, nurturing them and teaching peace. We can refuse to sacrifice another man's children as well, protesting war and living peace.

THERE IS NO "OTHER."

January 30

The transient Here seems to need and concern us strangely.
—Rainer Maria Rilke

The spiritual life is a demand for action. We may not, as we awaken spiritually, forget that compassion and love embrace life and the living rather than elude them. Compassion is not an idea. Humility is in walking with God and seeing her purpose, not in withdrawing and detaching from the pain of the world.

A man in his eighties, wise and earthy, once told a group of men to get up off their knees and put legs on their prayers. We cannot heal the earth by treating it as separate from us any more than we can heal our hearts by detaching from our joys and sorrows.

This does not mean that prayer and meditation are without substance. Does the monk praying in the distant mountain monastery affect the ways of war? Probably. Can the angry activist conspire with the corporate polluter? Perhaps. The engaged and compassionate heart heals truly.

CAN I FEEL THE EARTH BENEATH MY FEET AS I PRAY?

January 31

Mindful of my connection to the plant world, I can heighten my reverence for that world.

PLANT A TREE, A BUSH, A FLOWER, OR SOME HERBS TODAY.

February 1

This day marks the Feast of Saint Brigit—a celebration originating in the Celtic festival of Brigid, goddess of maidens, which evokes the movement into spring. The fifteenth of this month is Lupercalia, an ancient Roman festival honoring the sexual heat that permeates all of nature, and the twelfth is the Festival of Diana, the protector of wildlife and forest. It is also the time of Mardi Gras.

This is a period of turning outward from the inward focus of the winter months. We are celebrating the return of the light to the world, and the beginning of growth toward light of that which has thus far been blossoming in the dark.

We can use this month as a time of paying attention to how we manifest ourselves in the world.

February 2

God provides the wind, but man must raise the sails.
—SAINT AUGUSTINE

    Living the inner life in the world requires quite specific preparation. This spiritual power men are feeling is indeed "greater than ourselves." For some, this power is God, for others it is the power of reality. The mountains are a power greater than ourselves and possess just this power of things as they are. We don't set out to climb K2 in baggies and flip-flops. Rather, we study the way of the mountain; we listen to it and do all it tells us to do. Then we can blend with this great power.

🌿 🌿 🌿

IS MY CONCERN WINNING, OR MOVING?

February 3

Why is the special provenance of the masculine to heal the earth? It is not. Our unique task is to reclaim our power and our earthy heritage. This exhausted earth is the mirror of our exhausted spirit. Our vitality is siphoned off in the service of technology and the exploitation of the earth. Our worship has been shifted and we have been systematically gutted as we have gutted the earth. We have pissed on ourselves, drunk with progress, and drowned the oceans.

It is difficult to put an end to a war where there is no "other." The earth is not an enemy to be despised. Pogo named the enemy years ago. Us. And we are beginning to turn our backs on the masters of ruin. It is no easy task, taking responsibility and making amends, but only in facing it can our own vitality be restored. As the earth is healed, we are healed. Here is fruitful codependence, and here is the only acceptable future for our children.

❦ ❦ ❦

AS I TREAT MY ENVIRONMENT, SO I TREAT MYSELF.

February 4

The poet can know that the bear and the wolf sit just outside the campfire light and he can welcome them in as teachers.

We have lost our personal poetry in an age that demands reason and technology. As men grew into workers, justly providing for their families, we lost touch with that divine poet who could see a new carpet where others saw only an old rug, unchanged by imagination. Hurrying to the office, preoccupied by what lay ahead, the poems in our hearts faded. But the divine child, wondrous poet, explains to our hearts what the scientist can only describe to our minds. The poems we write, however we write them, in minutes we steal from reason, enlarge our world and fill it with wonder and knowledge. Our poems are part of our greater stories.

Each of us can write poetry. It is necessary to do so, to set aside a few moments a day to let the soul emerge and bring its message from the divine.

I CAN PRACTICE POETRY TO CLAIM MY LIFE.

February 5

I imagine, therefore I belong and am free.
—LAWRENCE DURRELL

Imagination has had a hard time of it. "It's just your imagination" means that whatever it is, it is not real. We have been told to stop imagining things, to get real, to stop being so dreamy. So we have dutifully gone along, leaving the creative play to children and poets, to the discredited dreamers and wacky artists so cruelly portrayed in mass media.

If this men's work means anything at all, it means that we are reclaiming our imaginations. It means that having a vision, culled from the divine and incarnated in action, is virtuous rather than laughable. Today it is possible to live imaginatively, supported by a community of poets and tricksters, and to feel a greater effectiveness and responsibility.

🌳 🌳 🌳

IMAGINE.

February 6

True ambition is not what we thought it was. True ambition is to live usefully and walk humbly under the grace of God.
—BILL WILSON

A man's purpose is revealed as he develops humility.

The word *humility* shares the same Greek root as the word *humus*—of the earth. So long as we are not grounded, not earthy, we are separated from the knowledge of our purpose. False ambition is driven by thirst and satisfied by consumption. We eat the earth rather than serving it. We teach hunger to our children. Anxiety and separation are our constant companions.

As we become grounded, we begin to see that we have all that we need and that the practice of gratitude and service will fill us more completely than all the meals and the malls we once worshiped.

WHAT'S THE "USE" OF WHAT I'M DOING?

February 7

Mindful of the grace of concentration and longing to recover my imagination, I can go within and find the poet.

WRITE A POEM TODAY.

February 8

*For every one who exalts himself will be humbled,
and he who humbles himself will be exalted.*
—LUKE 14:11

There is a blindness which comes with the satisfaction of our desires and ambitions. In a system that values getting over giving and doing over being, we are driven into a frenzy of accumulation which implies personal victory when satisfied. "Look what I did," we say publicly and privately. When we find that such things cannot last or that the satisfaction of one need leads only to another; when we find that we are only banging around in empty rooms, our despair can be great.

It is at this point that our hearts can begin to fill, rather than our endless guts. Here is where we pause and look at our mates, family, parents, community, and world and offer a word of gratitude for the great gifts they bring us. At this point, when the world of illusion has fallen away, if only for a moment, the road ahead is clear.

AM I RUNNING ON EMPTY, WITH THE ILLUSION OF A FULL TANK?

February 9

But when I breathe with the birds,
The spirit of wrath becomes the spirit of blessing,
And the dead begin from their dark to sing in my sleep.
—THEODORE ROETHKE

Pacman consumed. Pacman ate everything he encountered. If there was ever a pop icon of the Hungry Ghost this little pixel character was it. We can see ourselves easily in Pacman. Insatiable and wrathful, we kept gobbling and were increasingly diseased. Wrath followed easily when we were so disconnected from the source of blessing. Our disease increased, and our wrath grew, until finally we sought healing. In talks with other men, in prayer, in recommitment to the ways of religion in everyday life, we are healing old wounds and, in the process, healing our social and natural environment.

We can no longer deny connection, and as our healing continues, our awareness of connections grows more profound. We see we are connected to the dead as well as to the living. Our ancestors live in us and around us, informing our lives. We find courage and purpose in knowing we are not alone.

LIVING, CONNECTED, IN THIS VAST UNIVERSE BRINGS HUMILITY RATHER THAN FEAR.

February 10

Boredom is simply a lack of attention.
—CHRISTOPHER FREMANTLE

Consumed with consuming, we lost our minds.

Our senses were numbed by endless eating. Eyes, ears, and mouths were constantly busy, assaulted by our needs. We could not see, hear, or taste any longer. Our amusements were murdering us, and our food was becoming poison. Our hearts gave out too soon.

Boredom was not about having nothing to do, as we said. It was about not having enough to do. We mistook stimulation for activity. We felt dissatisfied when we were alone, away from our machines, or out of the audience.

In our process of healing, we regain the gift of attention. It is difficult to be bored when we hold still in the chaos, end our frantic busywork, and rejoice in the beauty of the present moment.

❦ ❦ ❦

PAYING ATTENTION IS A SMALL PRICE FOR THE GIFT OF THE PRESENT MOMENT.

February 11

The true teacher defends his pupils against his own personal influence. He inspires self-trust. He guides their eyes from himself to the spirit that quickens him. He will have no disciple.
—AMOS BRONSON ALCOTT

As children we looked for teachers and often found pedants and snake oil salesmen. We were not initiated and taught so much as we were indoctrinated. Schools, boy scout troops, and later for some the military taught the practical and infused doctrine. Our spirits were longing for freedom but we were taught the status quo. Initiation of men, by men, into the mysteries had become puny and dispirited.

As we move outward from narrow self-interests and take back our masculinity we can become initiators and teachers. We can say to our sons and to the boys in our communities that we value their spirits and their uniqueness. We can show them who we are rather than tell them who they should be.

❦ ❦ ❦

AS WE FREE OURSELVES FROM THE PATRIARCHY, WE BECOME FREE TO INVENT NEW RITUALS FOR THOSE WHO FOLLOW US.

February 12

Children are natural mythologists; they beg to be told tales, and love not only to invent but to enact falsehoods.
—George Santayana

Our educations were often incomplete. We were told to be big boys and not cry on our first days at school, so we didn't learn to grieve. When we told our tales of high adventure with wondrous creatures we were cautioned not to lie like that, so we didn't learn to use our imagination. When we said that we wanted to go climb mountains, we were asked if we were really, really sure, so we never learned faith in our intuition. Or to climb mountains.

WHAT GREAT ADVENTURE, REAL BECAUSE I SAY IT IS SO, WILL I LIVE TODAY?

February 13

Mindful of a power greater than myself and desiring to know it better, I can act humbly and remain open to ideas of my life that I may never have, alone.

WRITE A PRAYER.

February 14

Ecology is how to do Theology.
—James Park Morton

It is said elsewhere that the spiritual life is not a theory; we have to live it. There is no place for the disembodied way of life any longer. When we spend an hour in church on Sunday, or even thirty minutes each day in meditation and prayer, we are not meeting spiritual obligations; we are creating and reenforcing them.

When we accept healing the earth as one of our tasks as men, we are simultaneously accepting the path of spiritual observance. The earth is our most forceful reminder of the power of things as they are. It is, incarnate, the great spiritual energy that informs our lives. As we treat the earth, so we treat ourselves, and so we treat the gods. This trinity is holy. It demands our service.

WHAT OR WHO AM I SERVING TODAY?

February 15

The highest point a man can attain is not Knowledge, or Virtue, or Goodness, or Victory, but something even greater, more heroic and despairing: Sacred Awe!
—NIKOS KAZANTZAKIS

Consider what is sacred to you.

This is treacherous ground. We might slip away from this questioning by saying that we hold nothing sacred or, conversely, by claiming that our religious practices define what is sacred. Here, however, our quest is to find what we hold sacred right now, see what we want to see as sacred to us, and begin the practice of consciously acknowledging it.

We hold things, people, places, and enterprises sacred. That which engages is transcendental; impulse and energy are held sacred. That which informs our choices and activates our imaginations is what we hold sacred. That to which we bring our greatest intensity is sacred to us.

WHAT IS SACRED?

February 16

Men are accustomed to remembering their lives intellectually, and in the context of time and accomplishment. "Then, in 1956, I realized I needed to finish my studies and . . ." Such as this is only the husk of real information. As we begin this process of learning our stories and how to tell them, we have to jump to other methods, less rational and diagnostic, to put them together in new and vivid pictures, three-dimensional, with texture, odor, and color. In the present we need to become what Diane Ackerman calls "sensuists," rejoicing in sensual experience, and then to follow the thread of the senses into the past.

I remember still the smell of my mother's fur coat, and the heat of our car as we drove through the snowy streets of Berea, Ohio, in the winter of 1945. I can feel her coat against me—I was only three—and I can feel as well my father's hard knee moving against my feet as he worked the accelerator and brake. That smell is forever associated with the very first time I realized I was separate from the two of them. Those details make it real every time I remember.

WHAT ARE THE SENSUAL DETAILS OF MY STO

February 17

A mindful day.

This is a day of mindfulness. What is sought here is not a unique day, standing distinctly apart from all others, but a day when the practice of mindfulness moves into the foreground. Today is a day of enrichment and heightened awareness. Please bring this wonderful practice into every day.

Mindfulness is not an esoteric practice. Being mindful simply means being awake. For men, being mindful can mean the beginning of the end of the social masculine trance and the dismembered life. In mindfulness we become aware of the fullness and flow of our lives, one moment at a time.

The Appendix of this book contains specific directions and suggestions. I encourage you to visit a library or bookstore for additional help in this ancient practice. One excellent book is *Full Catastrophe Living* by Jon Kabat-Zinn, Ph.D. The Vietnamese Buddhist monk Thich Naht Hahn has written dozen   's, many of which concern mindfulness. M   es are *The Miracle of Mindfulness* and *Be-*

ful day. Please embrace it fully.

February 18

God is burning out of you everything which is unlike himself.
—MOTHER TERESA

In our journey we add on a great deal. We pick up stories from our families and the culture; we construct behavior and attitudes to simply keep on going. As we add and add, we are soon encumbered like a Beckett man, draped with layers of tattered clothing, rocks in our pockets, pebbles in our minds, and sleep in our eyes. The child we once were struggles on carrying all this weight, bewildered and confused with his sobs caught in his throat. We cannot easily shrug off this burden alone. We are much too attached to it. Yet we can begin to trust the process of transformation. As we are challenged by circumstances, perhaps leaving a lover or changing our work, or something far greater like the death of one we love, we can see each increment of this change as a caress from the divine hand, removing all that which stands between us and him.

As we become involved in the care of our souls, much will be burned away. Trust in the process is optional and we will often holler and clutch at that which is being removed. We will do this if we must but we must also remember that the process itself is not optional.

THIS PROCESS OF SOUL-MAKING REQUIRES ME TO TRUST IN
NOTHING AND TO HOPE FOR NOTHING.

February 19

Mindful of the need in my busy life to engage my spirit and acknowledge my soul, I will practice spending time in places where these needs can be met.

🌳 🌳 🌳

GO TO A CHURCH, TEMPLE, OR OTHER RELIGIOUS CENTER FOR AT LEAST THIRTY MINUTES OF CONTEMPLATION TODAY.

February 20

The man who never alters his opinions is like standing water, and breeds reptiles of the mind.
—WILLIAM BLAKE

Judgement, intolerance, and their wellspring, fear, inhabit us like tics, slowing our walk at every step. We are afraid, for example, that we might go spinning out of control. We might be annihilated by the unexplained or uncontrolled. So we create these great stories and theories of everything. Our personal grand unified theory that explains every phenomenon and justifies every action. These opinions, which is all they really are, form a protective bubble around us. Selective retention becomes a habit. Denial is immediate; when our beliefs are challenged, the process is easily short-circuited, and we are content to go on, unaltered, unchanged, unheeding, and incomplete.

When the irrefutable challenge finally comes, as it will, and our stories will not hold, we will break rather than bend. We will have lost all flexibility. Brittle and alone, we will crack up.

Men are learning now that this brittle and bitter man is a man of the past. The transformational man is of a newer generation, whatever his age. Acceptance and humility are real to him; a part of the practice of his life. The ebb and flow of life, the strength in the journey, are in his body and mind. He feels joy without inflation and deep pain without shattering. His story is his own.

🌿 🌿 🌿

DO I BEND OR BREAK?

February 21

> *God in us—entheos—enthusiasm;*
> *this is the essence of the holy madness.*
> —NORMAN O. BROWN

The transformational masculine is the spirited masculine. We are reclaiming the spiritual as the spiritual reclaims us. Our enthusiasm is being reborn.

We had become dis-spirited; "the spirit's gone," we said; "we've lost our spirit." We were spiritless in our living, loving, working, and ministering. In losing our spirit, we become detached . . . from the earth, the heart, and the hearth, as Sam Keen has put it. Spirit, earth, heart, hearth! All connected! We will not be transformed in a vacuum. This awakening happens in our entire body and mind. We cannot "think it through." The spirited man is spirited in all his pores and all his bones. His home is spirited, his loving is spirited, his people are spirited.

🌱 🌱 🌱

WHAT DOES THIS WORD **spirit** MEAN TO ME?

February 22

Secular "liturgy" is hardly the life of a child for most of us. Our colors of celebration dance in limited pixels on our TV screens; the music is of discord with our neighbors. We celebrate rarely. Our rituals are mundane.

When I go into the mountains with my children we ring a bell three times on entering the mountain or forest, and ring it two times again, followed by a bow to the mountain, after we have left. We are learning, the five of us, that the mountain is a special place, millions of years old only a few inches below the soil cover, covered with a rich variety of plants and trees and home to many creatures. Books do not tell us this. It is the ringing of that bell that teaches. The mountain would not be as holy for me without that bell and those children. I am the one who is jolted to life.

WE CAN INVENT TOGETHER A LITURGY OF EVERYDAY LIFE,
AWAKENING TO THE LIFE OF A CHILD,
WITH COLOR AND MELODY AND AWE.

February 23

. . . the only people for me are the mad ones, the ones who are mad to live, mad to talk, mad to be saved, desirous of everything at the same time, the ones who never yawn or say a commonplace thing, but burn, burn, burn like fabulous yellow roman candles exploding like spiders across the stars and in the middle you see the blue centerlight pop and everybody goes "Awww!"
—JACK KEROUAC

I bow to Bill, Larry, and Billy, good men who died too soon.

TODAY CONSIDER THE DEAD.

February 24

A mindful day.

This is a day of mindfulness. What is sought here is not a unique day, standing distinctly apart from all others, but a day when the practice of mindfulness moves into the foreground. Today is a day of enrichment and heightened awareness. Please bring this wonderful practice into every day.

Mindfulness is not an esoteric practice. Being mindful simply means being awake. For men, being mindful can mean the beginning of the end of the social masculine trance and the dismembered life. In mindfulness we become aware of the fullness and flow of our lives, one moment at a time.

The Appendix of this book contains specific directions and suggestions. I encourage you to visit a library or bookstore for additional help in this ancient practice. One excellent book is *Full Catastrophe Living* by Jon Kabat-Zinn, Ph.D. The Vietnamese Buddhist monk Thich Naht Hahn has written dozens of books, many of which concern mindfulness. My personal favorites are *The Miracle of Mindfulness* and *Being Peace*.

This is a beautiful day. Please embrace it fully.

February 25

We are born into a family and, at the last, we rejoin its full extension when gathered to the ancestors. Family grave, family altar, family trust, family secrets, family pride.
—JAMES HILLMAN

The family occupies us fully for years upon years. We are nurtured or abused, loved or ignored or probably parts of all of it. In a psychologized society we have learned to pathologize the family. Ask a man *who* he is and he is likely to tell you *what* he is, and often that demeaning what will center upon his family. "I'm the adult child of two alcoholics and *therefore* I . . ." We have put aside honoring our families in favor of blaming them and have thus cut ourselves off from our ancestors, both immediate and ancient. In remembering our lives, we can tell our families' stories. They are separate from our own and they are entangled with it. In honoring our ancestors by telling their stories we honor our own lives and continue the transformative process. We are not going back; we are going deep. The story of my great-uncle who pissed in a handkerchief and held it to his face to escape Nazi deathgas is my story as well. We are connected.

MY FAMILY LIVES IN ME AND IN MY STORY.

February 26

Mindful of my sources, I will put aside the phantom wounds and heal myself in the present moment. I can smile at my father right here, today, and know that, like me, he has felt pain and known joy.

February 27

We think that the ancestors are behind us, but they also go before us—a vanguard, a spirit wave, pulling us along.
—JOAN HALIFAX

The question is, can we get beyond the immediate pain of family to engage with a deeper understanding of where we are headed by seeing where we started. Can we let our family off the hook, let's say, in order to be able to connect with them and through them, with all the myriad creatures? The family information we carry with us can lead us in many directions, to every compass point of our souls, and to every direction of time.

As we continue to tell our family stories, as we go deeper into the truth of our being, it is difficult not to sense our other ancestors, darker and wilder. Somewhere a coyote lurks near an ancestral home, drawn by the smell of blood in the stew. In our veins we carry that moment of wildness. Knowing this we begin to know a greater family to whom we are responsible.

Our families precede us. We precede our children. We die to make room for them.

WHAT WILL MY LEGACY BE IN THE CHILDREN'S STORIES?

February 28

We look at each other; but we do not see each other anymore.
Our perception of the world has withered away;
what has remained is mere recognition.
—Viktor Shklovski

Not one of us is a category, a unit. There is a company chairman in book publishing who refers to people solely by their titles, that is, "you, editor," or "what about it, art director." Certainly he thinks this is efficient. Perhaps we have had enough of such cold and silly efficiency. And of such cold and silly men.

When we have failed to see our children, we have failed to educate them truly. Instead of allowing them to learn, we have instructed them. Instead of telling them stories, we have quizzed them on their "learning."

When we have failed to see our lovers, we have dishonored and objectified them.

Failing to see our families, we have amputated parts of our hearts.

Today we are learning to see. By our willingness to see ourselves, through story and sharing, we can see the people and the world around us.

IN HONORING OURSELVES, WE HONOR OUR PEOPLE
AND OUR HOMES.

February 29

In leap year, try to remember what you were worried about on this date four years ago. What were you happy about?

The vernal equinox is on the twenty first of this month. Spring begins and light and dark are equally balanced.

Ramadan, the Muslim month of fasting and purification, begins this month. Jews observe Purim, Buddhists celebrate spiritual community with Magna Puja, and the beginning of spring is honored by the Hindu celebration of Holi. For Christians, this is the beginning of the forty-day period of Lent, a time of penance and fasting prior to Easter.

March 2

A mindful day.

This is a day of mindfulness. What is sought here is not a unique day, standing distinctly apart from all others, but a day when the practice of mindfulness moves into the foreground. Today is a day of enrichment and heightened awareness. Please bring this wonderful practice into every day.

Mindfulness is not an esoteric practice. Being mindful simply means being awake. For men, being mindful can mean the beginning of the end of the social masculine trance and the dismembered life. In mindfulness we become aware of the fullness and flow of our lives, one moment at a time.

The Appendix of this book contains specific directions and suggestions. I encourage you to visit a library or bookstore for additional help in this ancient practice. One excellent book is *Full Catastrophe Living* by Jon Kabat-Zinn, Ph.D. The Vietnamese Buddhist monk Thich Naht Hahn has written dozens of books, many of which concern mindfulness. My personal favorites are *The Miracle of Mindfulness* and *Being Peace*.

This is a beautiful day. Please embrace it fully.

March 3

Make me a channel of thy Peace ...
—The prayer of St. Francis

For the next several days, we are going to consider this great prayer. As we recover our spiritedness we must be mindful of two important traps: one, the spiritual life is not a "thing" that we acquire, it is not material; and two, that we are not God, we must be willing to evaporate in order that a greater work can begin. The spirited man must avoid the trap of ego. In its opening phrase, this prayer says that we are willing to humble ourselves and that we are asking to be used for a purpose that we might not fully understand. We are asking that all our gifts be used and our liabilities removed in order that a message of peace will flow through us. It does not imply that we "go limp," that we bow our heads and acquiesce.

THE FIRE IN THE BELLY MUST BE STOKED
AND MUST BURN BRIGHTLY.

March 4

. . . that where there is hatred, I may bring love . . .

Love is the gift of an eager heart. It is a gift we give to ourselves as we give it to others. We give it away to keep it. Here we are asking for what we already have. Love sits waiting in our deepest places. The little boy we all were is loving. The spirited man is loving, with that little boy holding his hand and teaching him to enter every hating situation with love.

We are also praying here that we be empowered to be loving rather than simply to bear the gift of love. That is, we do not merely preach love, we are loving in our attitudes. Our children cannot hear the words we say about love if we do not practice it.

The practice of love is not limited. Who do we feel is not worthy of our love? Who is outside of the circle our love builds? Can we love our families but not love the family down the street? Are children in other lands not worthy of our love?

CAN I BUILD A CIRCLE OF LOVE THAT INCLUDES
RATHER THAN EXCLUDES?

. . . that where there is wrong,
I may bring the spirit of forgiveness . . .

Forgiveness is the gift of the open heart. It is through forgiveness that wounds are healed and the awful burden of the past cast off our shoulders. If we have been wronged and cannot forgive that, we are forever tied to the wrong. It is like leaning against a wall, rather than standing upright. Eventually you have to carry that wall everywhere you go. We are compulsively attached to blame and guilt. As we begin the practice of forgiveness, we can wear down the guilt compulsion. The spirited man is liberated by forgiveness, and those who follow, his children or his students, can be empowered by his model.

WE CAN "BRING THE SPIRIT OF FORGIVENESS" TO ALL WE DO.

March 6

... that where there is discord, I may bring harmony ...

There are times when we are achingly "out of synch," when the music of our lives and, it seems, the lives around us, grates and screeches. The universe is dissonant. We are lonely and anxious.

At such a time, we must restore our own harmonies and we can best do so by simply ceasing to fight the dissonance. This is the time to be in touch with our own truth, our own center. The outer world often seems messy. Frantic to fix it, we bring further madness. This is the time to quiet ourselves, to honor the impulse to heal the wounds of a pained world, and to reconnect with the melodies of peace and calm that play in us, sometimes so softly that we can barely hear them.

TO BRING HARMONY, BE HARMONIOUS.

March 7

. . . that where there is error, I may bring truth . . .

How afraid are we to go to the center of ourselves and find our truth there? Many men have been depressed for a long time, "in their male and resplendent selves" in D.H. Lawrence's words, because of the heavy errors they carry and that society carries. Is it true that a man is a money-making machine whose function is to provide "stuff" for his family? Is a man a failure if he isn't rich? It's easy to say we don't believe the money-maker myth, but look deeply. Is part of your error that in a secret and tender part of you, you believe that the accumulation of goods is what makes the man? What are the other errors in how we think about ourselves?

THE ONLY TRUTH WE CAN BRING IS OUR OWN. THERE IS NO
ARBITRATED TRUTH.

March 8

. . . that where there is doubt, I may bring faith . . .

This phrase suggests only that we bring faith, not resolution, not answers. We do not need to fix it. We do not need to remove the doubt. We are called, as men who have faith, to model it for those who are facing doubt. Zen teachers say that a student needs "great doubt, great faith, great effort." There is a liberating tension in the opposites, doubt and faith, which make gold, so we need to know that we only add, we do not diminish. We need to know as well that we are adding what is already there. That is, our personal evidence of the results of faith reveals the hidden faith of others. We are not accustomed to "mere" witnessing. So many men feel the need to reconstruct, replace, and remove that the notion of simply letting it be is mightily discomforting. We must realize that in bringing our experience of faith to those who doubt, we are revealing our hearts and honoring those we serve.

CAN I SHOW THAT I AM FAITHFUL RATHER THAN SAYING "HAVE FAITH"?

. . . that where there is despair I may bring hope . . .

Facing the despair of the world, in the community, in the face of a child, old before his time, is terribly difficult. It demands that we be willing to put aside our denial and our various drugs and feel that empty place deep in our bowels that is the habitat of our own fear and hopelessness. To feel the suffering of another opens the doors to that cavern with all its terrors. "Men Do" is our slogan. We cannot stand to see others suffer. We want to put an end to it at once, unbidden.

We have trained ourselves and been trained not to feel the pain. We have become desensitized and juvenilized in order to avoid the reality of despair. If we were truly awake, we would not be able to watch the eleven o'clock news without shuddering. We would not be able to read the newspaper without a cry of anger. Yet, as spirited men, we are called upon to shudder and to cry out against the pain. The images of despair surround us and force us to pay heed. We bring hope by being hopeful. When we finally face our own despair and find hope, we are charged with the task of bringing that hope to others.

BEING HOPE-FILLED IS PERSONAL, BUT IT IS NOT PRIVATE.

March 10

. . . that where there are shadows I may bring light . . .

Light falls freely and abundantly when obstructions are removed. We fear what is hidden in shadows and fail to see what stands before the light. Facing away from the source of light, we are in darkness, mystified by shadows. When we turn toward the light we can see the walls in front of it. Our battles are with the walls. The light will seek the farthest reaches of life when the source of shadow is destroyed.

Seeking enlightenment, we are enlightened. The shadows cast by fear and its companions, greed and self-ishness, are destroyed as our monolith of fear, fear of not being enough, fear of not having enough, begins to crumble before the light.

☙ ☙ ☙

THE LIGHT THAT BREAKS THROUGH SHINES ON THE ENTIRE FIELD OF OUR BEING AND BRINGS LIGHT TO ALL THOSE WE TOUCH.

. . . that where there is sadness, I may bring joy.

•

When the hearts of those we love have been broken by loss or when we see sadness in the faces of strangers, we must be cautious not to rob them of their feelings. We must bring joy rather than enforce joy. We must not confuse hilarity with joy. When a child's puppy dies, the child must be allowed to mourn that death. The joy we bring, then, is the strength of our own vulnerability, and the power of empathy.

AT TIMES OF SADNESS, THERE IS JOY IN KNOWING THAT ONE IS NOT ALONE.

March 12

Grant that I may seek rather ...
to understand than to be understood.

Daddy doesn't have to sit at the head of the table anymore. The enlightened man can assume a rightful place in his family without pomp or arrogance. The time of the patriarch is long past; those who try to perpetuate it are indulging in mockery and ugliness. Now we are learning to listen to the hearts of our families, our friends, and our communities rather than placing ourselves at their heads.

🌳 🌳 🌳

Is my understanding active?

March 13

Grant that I may seek rather ... to love than to be loved.

Being loved is a delicious and a passive state. Without it our spirits are diminished and our lives are filled with anxiety and thirst. Many men today long for their father's love. Others of us have spent years searching for a woman to do for us what we felt our mothers failed to do. We yearn for the warmth of our early years. A popular slogan says, "It's never too late to have a happy childhood."

Yes, it is.

As our spirits are nurtured through the rebirth of our instincts and our creative natures, our ability to love expands. As we begin to love others, actively and passionately, we begin to discover that we are lovable and that we are loved.

NURTURING, WE ARE NURTURED; TEACHING, WE ARE TAUGHT; LISTENING, WE ARE HEARD.

March 14

For it is by self-forgetting that one finds.

On the journey to the mature masculine we struggle to shed all the old bags of expectations, roles, and demands that restrict and enfeeble us. In the course of that peeling away of the layers of falsehood and dried skin, we finally meet ourselves. Some have the experience of seeing, for the first time, who they really are apart from the vision of others. For some, there is a realization of the true self, or the soul. By learning our own unique stories and by trying to live consciously, we arrive at the moment of seeing the self.

At just that point it is time to say "you're not so special, cowboy." We now can move from the unique to the communal. We see not our separateness, but our connectedness.

March 15

It is by forgiving that one is forgiven.

Helen Luke said, in an interview, "It is the break-through of forgiveness, in its most profound sense—universal and particular, impersonal and personal—that brings the 'letting go,' the ultimate freedom of the spirit."

When we cease blaming others, we begin to connect with them. When we cease blaming circumstances, we begin to live responsibly; when we cease blaming our fate, we are free to embrace it and to learn of its gifts.

WHO'S TO BLAME?

March 16

It is by dying that one awakens to eternal life.

    Use this enormous phrase as a meditation today. It contains worlds of riddles. What are they for you? It holds a solitary gem of wisdom. What is it for you?

    When I die, I hope that wildflowers will grow from my chest, and that my groin and head and feet will provide grass to protect the topsoil. I will my brain to the wolf pack and my heart to a child of a distant time. When I die, I leave space for Kamala and Willie. The Buddhist teachers tell me that when I was born, nothing was added, and that when I die, nothing will be taken away.

SHARE YOUR MEDITATION WITH ANOTHER MAN.

March 17

We are most deeply asleep at the switch when we fancy we control any switches at all.
—ANNIE DILLARD

The drunk tanks, psychiatric wards, emergency rooms, and doctor's offices are full of men who thought they had it all under control. The waiting rooms are filling up right now.

There is a man standing at the corner of Franklin and Pine, whose orderly life is about to be turned upside down by an autoworker in Japan whose wife had a headache all of last April.

The winds blowing across Lake Erie began in the beat of a butterfly's wing in Indonesia.

The assassin carries his weapon in a violin case.

My beautiful son carries Jellenik's disease, as did his paternal great-great-grandfather. As do I.

🌳 🌳 🌳

IF MY HAND IS NOT ON THE SWITCH, WHO IS PULLING IT?

March 18

A mindful day.

This is a day of mindfulness. What is sought here is not a unique day, standing distinctly apart from all others, but a day when the practice of mindfulness moves into the foreground. Today is a day of enrichment and heightened awareness. Please bring this wonderful practice into every day.

Mindfulness is not an esoteric practice. Being mindful simply means being awake. For men, being mindful can mean the beginning of the end of the social masculine trance and the dismembered life. In mindfulness we become aware of the fullness and flow of our lives, one moment at a time.

The Appendix of this book contains specific directions and suggestions. I encourage you to visit a library or bookstore for additional help in this ancient practice. One excellent book is *Full Catastrophe Living* by Jon Kabat-Zinn, Ph.D. The Vietnamese Buddhist monk Thich Naht Hahn has written dozens of books, many of which concern mindfulness. My personal favorites are *The Miracle of Mindfulness* and *Being Peace*.

This is a beautiful day. Please embrace it fully.

March 19

Before I can understand thy will *I must begin to see the illusion of* my will: *I must know as thoroughly as possible that my life consists of "I want" and "I want" and "I want."*
—CHARLOTTE JOKO BECK

We have lived in the turmoil and anxiety of our endless desires, our demands upon the lives of others, and our relentless demands upon ourselves. We have lived also in the box of other's desires of or for us. We have lived for "the next." Partner, job, city, drink, dollar, or day.

As we become men, spiritually connected, mature and responsive, we see the frailty of living a life of scrapping for the satisfaction of our demands. They will not be met or if met, they will fail us. Always.

As we grow from demanding to giving, the illusion continues to melt. Service to others reveals God. Seeking God reveals humanity. We cannot, in seeking the will of God, trip on our brother, homeless and stoned and lying in front of the restaurant door.

TODAY I WILL LOOK AT WHAT I HAVE BEEN GIVEN, WITHOUT ASKING, RATHER THAN WHAT I ASK FOR, WITHOUT GIVING.

March 20

Mindful of the source of my life, I can practice love and forgiveness where I have been resentful or where I have been silent. I can smile at my mother and see how she has felt pain and experienced joy.

WRITE A LETTER TO YOUR MOTHER TODAY.
MAILING IT IS OPTIONAL.

March 21

Forgetfulness of self is remembrance of God. Whoever knows God through God becomes alive, and whoever knows God through self becomes dead.
—ABU YAZID AL-BISTAMI

What can be done to forget the self? The religions of the world offer ways, the great libraries of the world hold books of counsel, men in our groups can offer advice. Once undertaken the journey to the remembrance of God cannot end.

No one is reading these words who has not begun that journey.

We have learned through men's work that something has been missing. We have called it by many names: creativity, commitment, spirit, imagination. We have not called it fame, success, recognition, riches. The shift in consciousness has already occurred.

Now we are seeing the destination.

TODAY I CAN SEE EVERY STEP I TAKE AS AN ARRIVAL.

March 22

You are not alone.
—Twelve-Step slogan

From the moment of consciousness, we see that we are surrounded by others; we hear, smell, taste, and feel them. We communicate with them in ways both gross and subtle. We make love and we wage private wars. These others are our partners, our enemies, our families, and our surrounding crowd. The problem for so many men has been that, entranced, we have been unconnected. We have felt friendless and loveless in the most intimate times.

The playboys made love only with their cocks. The "helpers" helped only with their ideas. The fathers parented only from their lairs. This was all we could do. It was all we knew how to do.

We know now that in our trances, our deep sleeps, we simply could not relate to one another authentically. We were "authenticated" by our work, our possessions (including women and children), our money, our masks.

As we awaken from the trance, we become embodied and spirited. The man wrapped in bandages, blind and unfeeling, is liberated to the true company of his fellows.

THE GREAT GIFT OF THE SPIRITUAL LIFE IS THE EXPERIENCE OF CONNECTION. YOU DO NOT HAVE TO BE ALONE. IN FACT, YOU CANNOT BE ALONE ANY LONGER.

March 23

God wants nothing of you but a peaceful heart.
—MEISTER ECKHART

Now we have awakened to our connectedness. Those old serpents, deep in the mind, which tell us that we don't belong, are twisting in their final agony. This is a time of great danger. Those ego dragons don't want to die. They don't want to give up control. So they will tell us anything to stay alive. This is a time of great peril; we must awaken to our illusions and seek the reality of our true selves, our souls.

Are we willing to take comfort in the simplicity of the spiritual life?

The old life, filled with "matters of great consequence," as the Little Prince pointed out, was killing us. We sought comfort and courage in every direction but in. Now the path, thought to be outward, is seen to be inward. Now the reason of science is replaced by the ambiguity of intuition. Now all our philosophy is replaced by our stories.

NOW ONLY PEACE IS DEMANDED.

March 24

Please curb your dogma.
—Graffiti

I often behave as if what I have to say is the received word. It isn't.

Out of fear and ignorance, I talk to my children rather than listening to them. When I am teaching, I am tempted to behave as if the path I am on excludes or, at times, obliterates the paths adjacent to it.

I am coming to the understanding that this cussed "opining" is one of the subtlest of barriers between myself and others. It is, therefore, a great barrier between myself and God.

🌳 🌳 🌳

TODAY I WILL LEAVE THE DOGMA CHAINED AND LISTEN DEEPLY TO
ALL THAT IS SAID.

March 25

"That reminds me of a story."
—Punch line of a cyber-joke in which
a computer is asked if it can think and
learn like a human being

We have forgotten our stories or, at least, have forgotten to tell them. Stories surround us, in books, movies, magazines, TV—"that story and more, right after this." "This" is yet another story, information often indistinguishable from the stories of doom and politics that precede and follow it. We are so immersed in narrative that there doesn't seem to be time to learn our own stories, to learn from our own stories, and to pass those stories on, a heritage of what happened close up. We need the comfort of our own stories, the continuity of our own narrative, and the knowledge of our own lives, separate and unique.

Those who need to learn from us will learn far more from our stories than from our opinions and ideas. What is remembered is what happened far more than what we thought about what happened. Events and feelings carry masses of information beyond what the mind can order.

OUR STORIES ARE CARRIED IN OUR HEARTS AND BODIES AND WE
NEED TO LEARN TO TELL THEM FROM THERE.

March 26

Mindful of the power of my ancestors, I can connect with them in the present moment to enrich and deepen my daily life.

WHAT IS YOUR PATERNAL GREAT-GRANDFATHER'S FULL NAME?

March 27

I will tell you something about stories,
(he said)
They aren't just entertainment.
Don't be fooled.
They are all we have, you see,
all we have to fight off
illness and death.
—LESLIE MARMON SILKO

Our stories heal and protect us. They shelter us from the ways of harm. We need to build them well, sometimes with pain, always with honesty. They provide knowledge of our uniqueness and awareness of our commonality. They will tell us where we have come from, where we are, and where we are going—if we pay attention to them.

Consider your story. How much of it do you know?

How much do you know of the stories of your parents? Their parents? Do you know the stories of your community? Do you know the stories your friends have lived? Do you know the true story of your nation?

TODAY IS A DAY OF STORY-TELLING . . . YOUR STORY.

March 28

It is, after all, not man but the universe that is subtle.
—Barry Lopez

As we grow in spiritual consciousness, we must beware the trap of feeling unique in our awareness. This "spiritual materialism," or a blindness to the gifts freely given to all sentient beings, will only reinforce the very self-centeredness and isolation that has caused us pain for so long. It is our part to participate in the arising of the natural world, and to deny its abundant metaphysical power is to continue to attempt to dominate it. The consequences of the denial of the spirit in nature surround us.

Now we can work with the joy of deepening understanding of the great web of life, mysterious and often savage. The wolf who honors his prey and the caribou who offers his life are our teachers.

AM I SUFFERING FROM SPECIALNESS?

A mindful day.

This is a day of mindfulness. What is sought here is not a unique day, standing distinctly apart from all others, but a day when the practice of mindfulness moves into the foreground. Today is a day of enrichment and heightened awareness. Please bring this wonderful practice into every day.

Mindfulness is not an esoteric practice. Being mindful simply means being awake. For men, being mindful can mean the beginning of the end of the social masculine trance and the dismembered life. In mindfulness we become aware of the fullness and flow of our lives, one moment at a time.

The Appendix of this book contains specific directions and suggestions. I encourage you to visit a library or bookstore for additional help in this ancient practice. One excellent book is *Full Catastrophe Living* by Jon Kabat-Zinn, Ph.D. The Vietnamese Buddhist monk Thich Naht Hahn has written dozens of books, many of which concern mindfulness. My personal favorites are *The Miracle of Mindfulness* and *Being Peace*.

This is a beautiful day. Please embrace it fully.

March 30

> *Paradoxically, what we most have in common*
> *may be the stuff we hide from each other.*
> —LETTY COTTIN POGREBIN

Confession is good for the ratings. Emotional exhibitionism and the sentimental jackals hosting psycho–talk shows pollute the airwaves.

Beneath the secrets we no longer keep is a greater one that drives our lives. Secrets feed shame and are fed by them. It is not, for example, as important to know that I stole as it is to know the feeling of inadequacy that led me to steal. We are learning that telling all of the facts of our behavior can serve as a cover-up for the shame that drives us. Men are beginning to understand that reserve and prudence are virtues. We are telling each other our feelings rather than shoveling shit about our actions.

Perhaps one of our deepest shared secrets is our shame. Perhaps we are looking for friends to talk to, one-on-one, about the shame our secrets carry. The spirited man is not interested in confessors or vast audiences of empathizers. We seek intimacy rather than exposure.

🌳 🌳 🌳

WHAT AM I HIDING?

March 31

In the archer there is a resemblance to the mature person. When he misses the mark, he turns and seeks the reason for his failure in himself.
—CONFUCIUS

Remembering our lives and learning our stories is a matter of great urgency. It is important that it not be an exercise in blame and self-pity. Close attention to our stories will always reveal our complicity in events or our reaction to those things we could not control which led to "failure."

Shit happens.

Grace happens.

WHAT'S HAPPENING?

April 1

A rich month. For Buddhists, on the fifth, there is the feast of Avalokistesvara, the bodhisattva of compassion, and in the Zen tradition, there is the celebration of the Buddha's birthday on the eighth. On the thirteenth there is the ancient Roman festival of Ceres, celebrating the agricultural season. This is the time of Passover or Pesach, and in India, it is the time of Kalpa Vruksha, the festival of spring. In the Christian world, this is the time of the passion of Christ and the celebration of his resurrection.

The earth is coming exuberantly alive, transformed by heat and light. This month can be a month of vitality. Men can practice resurrection. The spirited masculine is called to shield and protect the earth now. The task is to begin again husbanding the earth, heeding its call and celebrating its life.

If I am not for myself, who is for me? And if I am only for myself, what am I? And if not now, when?
—HILLEL

Many men have led lives of dominating and abusing others because they felt so poorly about themselves. Others of us thought that taking care of ourselves meant being selfish or self-indulgent. Frightened by fantasies of inadequacy, we accumulated cars and watches and clothes and toys and said we were being "for ourselves," when in fact, we were denying ourselves.

In learning to be truly for ourselves, we awaken to the reality of community.

IN AWAKENING TO THE REALITY OF COMMUNITY, WE ARE SWEPT INTO MOVEMENT.

April 3

The catalogue of phrases, words, even tones of voice that will shut down my nervous system is vast. My wife only has to answer my talk with silence and I can feel my scalp crawl. Soon enough I will have a headache, my shoulders will be like wood, and the high-pitched, low-decibel scream in my ears will obliterate every word that might follow the silence. Chaos follows, within and without.

Listening to ourselves listen is a delightful and difficult task. Communication is so often ended when our bodies fight our minds' battles. As we become fully engaged in the moments of our lives, we become more alert to the old mechanisms of disengagement. It is also important to see that they are being dismantled simply by a fearless commitment to openness and honesty.

WHAT DO I HEAR WHEN I LISTEN DEEPLY TO MY BODY?

April 4

A mindful day.

This is a day of mindfulness. What is sought here is not a unique day, standing distinctly apart from all others, but a day when the practice of mindfulness moves into the foreground. Today is a day of enrichment and heightened awareness. Please bring this wonderful practice into every day.

Mindfulness is not an esoteric practice. Being mindful simply means being awake. For men, being mindful can mean the beginning of the end of the social masculine trance and the dismembered life. In mindfulness we become aware of the fullness and flow of our lives, one moment at a time.

The Appendix of this book contains specific directions and suggestions. I encourage you to visit a library or bookstore for additional help in this ancient practice. One excellent book is *Full Catastrophe Living* by Jon Kabat-Zinn, Ph. D. The Vietnamese Buddhist monk Thich Naht Hahn has written dozens of books, many of which concern mindfulness. My personal favorites are *The Miracle of Mindfulness* and *Being Peace*.

This is a beautiful day. Please embrace it fully.

April 5

We are each so much more than what some reduce to measuring.
—KAREN KAISER CLARK

We are accustomed to measuring ourselves and being measured by others to determine our worth. In the locker rooms we checked every cock we could see; in school our grades determined our worth; and the opinions, real or imagined, of family and lovers often set the course of our days now.

Social pundits provide measures as well. They reduce us to fit a narrow mold. We are told our families are "dysfunctional," for example, as if a family is a spiritless piece of machinery, a clock perhaps, that chimes well or not at all.

It is insanity to think that we don't measure well on scales that measure poorly.

We are learning, as spiritual men, that it's the scales that are dysfunctional. Who can measure the expansion of the heart at the smile of a child? What measure is there for the sorrow at death in war or for anger at war itself? The heart cares little for measuring.

WHEN I FALL INTO THE TRAP OF SEEING MYSELF AS ONLY A MACHINE, I VOW TO LAUGH AND FEEL THE MYSTERY OF MY LIFE.

Mindful of my ancestors I can receive their teachings here today.

WHAT IS YOUR PATERNAL GREAT-GRANDMOTHER'S MAIDEN NAME?

April 7

Where did I lose you, my trampled fantasies?
—ANDRÉ DE RICHAUD

As we have grown and changed, moved from place to place and person to person, we have left behind little bits of ourselves in the dreams and plans that were never fulfilled. It is important to look at these as we recover our full masculinity. The roads we didn't take constitute amputations from the full self, and we often carry secret grief for the missing pieces. Lenny Holzer says that a feeling buried is buried alive. So as we recover the past and bring our feelings into consciousness, we enliven the present and empower the future.

The question above is positive. It is not a prompt for self-pity or shame but instead a goad to examine the past and see what was lost for good and what for ill. We are not asking where we went wrong. We are exactly where we need to be. We are simply asking how we got there and what happened along the way.

❦ ❦ ❦

IT'S NEVER TOO LATE TO RUN AWAY AND JOIN THE CIRCUS.
IT'S NEVER TOO LATE TO CHOOSE, VIGOROUSLY,
TO PUT ASIDE CHILDISH THINGS.

April 8

I will not cut my conscience to fit this year's fashions.
—LILLIAN HELLMAN

It is the eco-fashion in some circles to refuse to buy Japanese cars, or to eat ice cream that contains pieces of the rain forest. The first is probably a good idea, but what is the value to the children in our own neighborhoods who still breathe the polluted air from other cars that we drive rather than using available public transportation? We need to boycott our egos and our fears.

Men are seeing that the old way—displaying one's self-worth on the wrist, on the back, or in the driveway—was vain and silly. What was once fashionable is now regarded as pathetic. We must beware, however, of mindlessly adopting the new stances. The spirited man is led by compassion, not fashion. We can begin to think and to act from the point of view of our ancestors rather than our neighbors. We act to serve those we will never see, rather than to impress those who see through us.

LOOKING DEEPLY, I CAN BE ASSURED OF TAKING
THE APPROPRIATE ACTION.

April 9

When I am holding my son against my chest, murmuring and making whispery sounds into his hair and neck, I am not revealing or acting out of my "feminine side." That man, holding that boy at that moment, is the whole complex mass of skin, flesh, bones, and blood that gives me form and consciousness. There is not some side of me that sashays out of the dressing room to coo to my little boy and then quickly disappears, leaving me to take my seat at the head of the table.

We are beginning to hurl ourselves into our lives, wholeheartedly, holding nothing back, willing to be burned to a cinder by the time the gig is up. Men are owning their gentleness, softness, and vulnerability rather than disembodying these qualities as if they were a foreign being come to roost. "Oh, that's my inner woman. She'll be gone shortly."

It's a relief for men to love their children freely and openly. It is our responsibility to own that love in the same fashion.

MY MASCULINITY IS GENTLE AND SOFT.

April 10

In the beginner's mind there are many possibilities;
in the expert's mind there are few.
—SHUNRYU SUZUKI

In the practice of meditation, my ideas of meditation are barriers. In spirited living, all my ideas about spirited living choke me and hold me halfway between the ground and the sky. Just so, in spirited fathering my ideas about fathers are barriers. When I am listening to my son with my ideas whirling—who he should be, what he should do, why I'm so inadequate—then I am listening to all my ideas and my son is left outside the door, without a teacher. And I am alone as well, teacherless.

I am learning to face each day, each situation, as a beginner, eager for help and uncertain of the outcome.

TODAY IS A DAY FOR BEGINNERS.

April 11

There is a beautiful cathedral uptown in Manhattan. It has been in the process of construction and renovation for longer than seems at all necessary. The facade seems always to have scaffolding obscuring the scowling gargoyles and statues of saints and church fathers. Workmen and stonemasons practice their craft daily. The south portico is rising, one stone at a time. Inside, lit by a magnificent rose window, is a constantly changing exhibit of sacred and secular art. There are pieces permanently installed as well; a wolf sculpture by Kappy Wells stands near a monument to New York City fire fighters. The growth of this place is slow to the eye of a worried man accustomed to rapid change. But rapid change leaves little time for contemplation or, just as importantly, for mourning.

In creating change, whether in our environment or our hearts, we need to take the time to listen to the wisdom the place or the heart contains.

The Cathedral of Saint John the Divine will never be "finished," but its prudent pace of growth gives it, at every moment of its process of being, great spiritual strength and comfort.

THERE IS NO DECISION TO BE MADE TODAY THAT CANNOT BE PUT OFF UNTIL TOMORROW.

April 12

Many could forego heavy meals, a full wardrobe, a fine house,
et cetera; it is the ego they cannot forego.
—MOHANDAS GANDHI

During the children's rebellion of the mid-1960s there
was a lot of talk about "destroying the ego." Popular songs
lauded this idea, and the popular culture mandated it.
Many man-boys set about to do so with great vigor. Those
who made it through this exercise discovered a great reality. You can't destroy what you don't have.

We've grown up now, "the children of the future,"
and find ourselves encumbered with much too much bag-
gage. We have filled that bag we drag along beside us with
the expectations of others, our own dead dreams, and our
fears of the future. Our egos have become the source of
suffering.

WHO IS THIS "I" WHO IS HURTING ME SO?

April 13

I just don't want all this to be a posthumous pleasure.
—Anonymous

Not one of us is so enlightened or likely enough to become so that we don't wish to see the results of our service.

A man, in building his life, his family, his work will face grave problems of endurance and faith. As he becomes awakened and able to express his own spirit and his great love and commitment to his bliss, the load becomes lighter. As he becomes liberated from his own fears, he is able to see the joy in the eyes of the children and families or communities he has served. He was served, is served, not so much by faith, as by patience and honesty.

In moving along a spiritual path, we'd best move slowly and keep our minds right about our motives. It's far better to say truthfully that you want to see the fruits of your labors now, and be judged by others, than to say dishonestly that you are interested only in the eternal and know yourself that you are lying.

Is this "men's work" just another possession?

When the voices of children
are heard on the green
And laughing is heard on the hill,
My heart is at rest within my breast
And everything else is still.
—WILLIAM BLAKE

   Listen to children laugh today. Contrast that with the laughter you hear from adults. We have learned how to laugh, in fact we can recognize each other by our distinctive laugh sounds. Some chortle, some explode, some snort wetly.

   A child's laugh erupts from her entire body and mind. When a child is laughing at a circus clown's pratfall, there is some of the pratfall in the laugh. A child's laugh is without pretense; it is often decidedly unsociable. The laughter of many grown men is only pretense and is often only sociable. We suffer from "laughter debt." If you doubt this, think about the times when you have laughed yourself weak and breathless over some truly small joke. My children still talk about the time that I laughed, rolling on the floor and gasping for air, over a belch joke in a comic movie. It had been too long since I had laughed.

WHAT'S SO FUNNY?

April 15

Mindful of the need to observe my life in process, I will take occasional glimpses at the little truth about myself. I can see my story all around me.

<small>Empty your wallet. Create an autobiography using what you find there.</small>

April 16

Without heroes, we are all plain people
and don't know how far we can go.
—BERNARD MALAMUD

Who are those people who, by the example of their lives, inspire admiration and emulation? One type of hero comes from the media—comic books, television, or radio plays—depending on your age.

As little boys, we imitated, with all our imagination, cowboys, superheroes, or athletes. We wore capes or made swords of sticks and conquered all who would oppose us. It is worthwhile today to take a look at how completely we became those others as we tried out all the roles available to us.

For today, remember sensually the great absorption into those types of heroes. In quiet time, reenter that world of endless creativity of the small boy. Smell the smells on the imaginary fields or mountains. Hear the sounds nearby and far away that were either included or denied. Feel the warmth of the sun and the touch of invented tools or weapons. This is a few minutes of remembering our lives. Give this gift to yourself today.

MY HEROES ARE MY ANCESTORS AND TEACHERS.
I WILL LEARN TO HONOR THEM.

April 17

Man cannot live by bread alone. He must have peanut butter.
—Brother Dave Gardner

If there is a particular significance to this quote, it has entirely evaded me. Find whatever it is you need in it.

It is here as a reminder that we men have the God-given right to be silly from time to time. Many of us pursued career, college, relationships, and the accumulation of things with fierce zeal. We took the bits in our teeth and set out to conquer every playing field.

Now that we have awakened to the call to service and selflessness, it's time to lighten up. Not one of us can be of much long-term use if we burn ourselves out in unfocused zealotry. "More spirituality" is a self-defeating need.

Today, and more often, consider the delight of silliness. Dare to be preposterous.

April 18

A hero is a man who does what he can.
—ROMAN ROLLAND

I had a great-uncle, Uncle Lacy, who was a hero to me. He was a farmer, a bachelor, a horseman, and a bigot. He died in 1959, of a broken heart. My grandmother had died earlier in the year and the loss was too great for him.

When I was a young boy, Uncle Lacy taught me to ride, milk cows, and herd sheep with the help of our dogs Cam and Lady. Uncle Lacy could spend all day in the saddle, back straight and hand easy on the reins. When one of the other workers would bring ice water out to the fields in the late afternoon, Uncle Lacy never took any. He always said, "I had some water this morning."

In the evenings he would call me into his room to listen to *Amos and Andy* on the radio. I knew in my heart that there was something wrong about that program and about what he said about black people, but I forgave him. His room smelled of chewing tobacco and the dust just outside the screen door. I just needed to be in there with him.

UNCLE LACY HAD A SAMPLER IN HIS ROOM. IT SAID:
"A FRIEND IS NOT A PERSON
WHO IS TAKEN IN BY SHAM
A FRIEND IS ONE WHO KNOWS OUR FAULTS
AND DOESN'T GIVE A DAMN."

April 19

Disciples do owe unto masters only a temporary belief and a suspension of their own judgement till they be fully instructed, and not an absolute resignation or perpetual captivity.
—FRANCIS BACON

If our heroes become our teachers, we must hope they understand that the relationship must end. Too much dependence on another leads to atrophy rather than growth. We need to let them teach and then let them go. The relationship has to change if we are not to get stuck. When the so-called men's movement first found its legs, some men became the teachers, most of us became willing students. They had opened up their hearts to us. Now we have seen many of these men move to the background and we must honor them for having such grace.

If we are fortunate, we have had a few good teachers in our lives and will have more. If we look at who our teachers are today we can see where we have come; when the time comes to let them go, we will know where we are headed.

❦ ❦ ❦

WHO ARE MY TEACHERS?

April 20

Every man has a house-broken heart except the great man.
—DJUNA BARNES

No house will break our hearts. How we feel about the house can snap us like twigs.

When it is time to make a home, resistance deadens the heart. It is difficult to grow into the reality of caring for a home if we have bought the myth of the free man, always on the road. There is a time for that freedom just as there is a time for the greater freedom of home and, if it is our destiny, family.

Settling into place, our hearts can expand. The heart will break if we are always glancing, furtively, at the closed door. The heart will break also if we fail to understand that our homes are resting places for the spirit. The frights of the day evaporate at the hearth. This is a powerful force, this homemaking, and men have resisted it to their peril for years.

THE SPIRITED MAN BUILDS A HOME ABOUT HIM,
SLOWLY AND REFLEXIVELY.

April 21

Humility has its origin in an awareness of unworthiness, and sometimes too in a dazzled awareness of saintliness.
—COLETTE

The teacher says to the student, "Don't tell me, show me!" Who we are is unmistakable and often quite different from who we say we are.

It is remarkable and invigorating to awaken to a life of service, spirit, and earthiness. When we see the images of the earth from space or when we really watch the children grow, we are reminded of our own humble state.

We need to beware at this point of the old masculine ego, still muscular and only slightly out of condition. It will shove its way into the room, upset the table lamp, and start talking about how great it is to be so humble.

☙ ☙ ☙

EACH DAY WE NEED TO LOOK OUTWARD TO SERVE AND INWARD FOR GRATITUDE. AND WE NEED TO BE CAREFUL NOT TO SWITCH THE DIRECTION WE'RE LOOKING.

My ancestors live on in me. I deepen my daily life by mindful attention to the ancestors.

FIND OUT WHERE A GREAT-GREAT-UNCLE IS BURIED.

April 23

For me, the word "warrior" and all of the martial images need to be stopped. I don't want to renovate or spiritualize them. . . .
They are degrading metaphors, the ones that damaged us.
—SAM KEEN

We hear talk about men as the "peaceful" or the "spiritual" warriors. The metaphors of war and its soldiers are all around us, they crowd up against our thinking, creating chaos. Men were assigned this role and continued to play it long after its utility had evaporated. The role creates a mind set of antagonism, "us versus them," "the good guys" versus the black hats (or the yellow peril, the drug kingpins, women, the cultural elite—the list is endless).

Today we can question the myth of the warrior. Is it time to retire the idea of man as warrior, no matter what we consider the war to be? Must men speak of being spiritual warriors? Isn't there some other way to say that we are spirited and engaged without the metaphor of the war-making man? For today we can consider other words than warrior, in the hope of ending the *social* myth. For one, we could say instead that we are spiritual fathers. There are others.

IF WE WON'T BE CALLED WARRIORS ANYMORE,
WHAT WILL WE BE CALLED?

April 24

In the infancy of humankind, war was a practical, deep-gutted impulse toward preservation. We were tuned to make war much as we were tuned to hunt. Men made war then. In very recent times we have been haunted by the spectacle of boyish old men, not of warrior age, parading in war garb and killing "cleanly." This injures our national and individual psyches, this charade of old and putatively wise men behaving like young men, shaking their guns. We can more easily see and pity the female counterpart, the old woman painted and dressed like a teenager, smiling with palsied lips at every passing stranger. These are not the models our children need.

Our spirits suffer as we continue to do war. We see young boys, unmentored and unloved, sent away by the boyish men to be warriors before they were taught to be men.

For today let's say we won't play war anymore. Men can say that if you want to fight a war against something or someone, go get your soldiers someplace else. Men can say that if you want change, you're going to have to find another way to talk about it.

PEACEMAKING IS AN INSIDE JOB.

April 25

However rare true love may be, it is less so than true friendship.
—Francois La Rochefoucauld

In the beginning of this putative men's movement, men were moving all over the map. We were drumming in Berkeley, being Wild Men in Texas, and mapping our psyches in workshops across the country. Some men insisted that this was a political movement, others prayed it would never become such.

The drums are quieter now and the masks hang on our walls. Many of us are beginning to hear a quiet voice that says I just want a friend or maybe two. Disconnected from our selves, we were disconnected from each other. A member of my men's group recently said that all he really wants is to be able to put his head on someone's shoulder. Another man said that his wife was his best friend and that he wasn't sure that was such a good idea.

What is it to be a friend to another man? It means listening with the whole mind. It means being willing to suffer. It requires sacrifice, repentance, and forgiveness. It means being able to be quiet with him.

WHAT IS IT TO BE A FRIEND TO ANOTHER MAN?

April 26

Knowledge is power. Unfortunate dupes of this saying will keep on reading ambitiously, till they have stunned their native initiative, and made their thoughts weak.
—CLARENCE S. DAY

We read the newspapers, watch the eleven o'clock news right before bed, read journals and books in our fields, scan CD-ROMs to check the facts, and do our best to stay informed so we won't let the world slip by unnoticed. The result is—the world slips by unnoticed.

We can become alive by playing with children, talking with friends about the shape of that cloud up there or the smell of a cheeseburger, or by simply sitting and observing our breath. Exercising our senses and our imaginations can awaken our thinking and our intuition.

What if the morning paper was recycled unread just for today? What if the TV or radio were not turned on today, and books were left untouched? What knowledge and power would be lost and what would be gained?

I WILL NOT MISS MY APPOINTMENT WITH MY OWN LIFE TODAY.

April 27

When I see myself as the problem,
I have made myself into an object
—CHARLOTTE JOKO BECK

We hear it all too often: "I just realized that I'm the problem, not . . . (my wife, my father, my boss, my neighbors)." Not so. This has the sound of a great breakthrough and the birth of humility when in fact it is an exercise in doing to ourselves what we have so long done to others.

Our families are not machines, which become "dysfunctional" subject to tinkering; our relationships cannot be "fixed" like some cheap toy, and not one of us is "the problem" in our own lives.

That leaves a blistering koan.

WHAT'S THE PROBLEM?

April 28

Each blade of grass has its spot on earth whence it draws its life, its strength; and so is man rooted to the land from which he draws his faith together with his life.
—JOSEPH CONRAD

Each man in the course of his life is faced with the reality of exile. In younger years, in springtime, this is where we belong; just around the corner and absolutely alone, without God or friend to stand by. It is inevitable. Not as certain is the return from exile, in later years, in early winter.

This exile is from the land, from God, and from our own true nature. We have often found the exile to be comfortable. Alcohol and other drugs take us into exile, as do work and love. Consuming madly and frantically, seeking to be "entertained" exiles us, pushing us through the door with silken hands.

AM I IN EXILE? IS IT TIME TO RETURN?

April 29

*Men fall into a routine when they are tired and slack; it has all
the appearance of activity with few of its burdens.*
—WALTER LIPPMANN
Revolution and Culture

Sameness in our days is compelling. Habit and routine
are comforting, to be sure, and certainly there is a deeply felt
need for routine and predictability. Yet we live now in a culture where the routine of work and the absorption into entertainment occupy fully two-thirds of every waking day. We
escaped our own deeper realities and broke our hearts in the
process. The spirit suffers greatly as imagination is crushed
by imitation and repetition. We have thought that the outside
world was too threatening so we have fled into our family
rooms and out of our families. The *Today Show* became the
noisy replacement for the ancient tradition of quiet prayer
and meditation at the start of a new day. We thought we
were alive when we were really entranced.

As we became aware of the emptiness in the center of
our beings that would not be filled or comforted by any routine, our spirits awoke. Now each day is a fresh opportunity
to care for the spirit. The invaluable time we spend now in
quietness and solitude or in intimacy with our mates has
quickened the unfolding of the spiritual life. Our minds are
less filled with chatter and the crust around our hearts has
crumbled a bit.

AM I ABLE TO FIND THE TIME TO LOOK DEEPLY OR AM I STILL
SPREAD TOO THIN?

April 30

Inside each of us is a baby we have to protect. This baby is all future generations. . . .
—THICH NHAT HANH

Here we meet, at last, the true "inner child." Here we learn that to care for this baby is to care for all babies of all generations to come. Thich Nhat Hanh says that to take care of this baby is to take care of everything.

We cannot destroy the forests and take care of this baby. We cannot pollute the air and take care of this baby. This baby is not cared for by us when we harm others or when we harm ourselves. This baby we carry does not need our anger, our addictions, or our greed. The greatest care we can give this baby is the sweetest care we give ourselves.

Today, we can live "as if" that baby we carry is at the center of our awareness. Our protection and care of this baby can be reflected in every action we take today. We can ask ourselves, "How does this (transportation, work, conversation, food, etc.) affect the child I am carrying?"

SPEND A FEW MOMENTS GETTING TO KNOW THE BABY YOU ARE
CARRYING AND THEN TAKE HER INTO YOUR DAY.

May 1

May first, May Day, has been known for centuries as *Beltane*, halfway between the spring equinox and summer solstice, the point of fertility and beauty.

This is the month of Wesak, celebrating the birth and enlightenment of the historic Buddha; of Shavuot, the giving of the Torah; and of the Ascension.

On the eighteenth is the Greek celebration of the Festival of Pan, the god of the flocks, the Herdsman. He is symbolized by the phallus and was considered a god of fertility. Legend says that on the day of Christ's crucifixion, the cry "Great Pan is dead" was heard in the Ionian Sea and that from that moment the voices of the oracles were silent.

A month of caretaking, fecundity, and eroticism. A deeply masculine time.

May 2

Religion is what we do with our solitariness.
—ALFRED NORTH WHITEHEAD

When I begin to confront my aloneness, I am confronted as well with the spiritual demand for community. In the past, both my solitariness and my need for others were so frightening that I turned my head. The consequence of that denial was that I became *disspirited*. I could fantasize but I could not hope. I could talk to God but, without the voices of others, I could not hear God's answers.

Although I may develop a personal relationship with a power greater than myself, that relationship cannot grow if I demand that it be a private one. If I build walls to protect my solitariness, then my spirit is at great peril.

Now I am learning to touch others, to listen closely when they speak. There is purposeful ritual in my life, directed to connection rather than separation. I share my feelings as well as my thoughts. The spirit, the aliveness, is awakening.

I CANNOT HOPE ALONE.

May 3

I am made not only of people but of places. Searching mindfully for the places in my extended story, I enrich my life and my community.

FIND, ON A MAP, THE PLACE WHERE YOUR MATERNAL GRANDMOTHER WAS BORN.

May 4

We have forgotten the beast and the flower not in order to remember either ourselves or God, but in order to forget everything except the machine.
—JOSEPH WOOD KRUTCH

We have lived at risk of estrangement from the beast and the flower for many years. We treated manufactured environments such as zoos, botanical gardens, and whatever-Worlds as acceptable substitutes for the real one just beneath our feet. We substituted voyeurism for awe and wonder. The technology that brought us images of the natural world became more important than the world itself.

Now we are learning that in trivializing and sentimentalizing our environment, we had diminished our ability to revere it. Now we are discovering that there is no end to beauty and wonder in our own backyards or in the park just down the block. We are becoming enraptured by our true environment, muddy and buggy as it is, and breaking the hypnotic hold of the environment as entertainment, perfect and always moving, in harmony, just so, with the piped-in music and the cadre of explainers.

ψ ψ ψ

IS THE SCENT ON THE BREEZE TOO PERFECT?
WHERE IS THE SMELL OF SHIT?

May 5

"Love or perish" we are told, and we tell ourselves. The phrase is true enough so long as we do not interpret it as "Mingle or be a failure."
—PHYLISS MCGINLEY

Let's not be fooled by our tendency to hang out together. Thoreau pointed out that even pigs huddle, just to keep warm.

We men were great social critters—we could hoist a grilled shrimp on a toothpick with the best of them. We celebrated religious holidays with great pomp and, if we were liberated, went to PTA meetings and joined school committees.

Now, in our men's groups or with friends and families, we are going deeper. Our feelings have become part of our social repertoire and many of us are skipping the cocktail get-togethers and the tailgate parties, not because we think there's anything particularly wrong with them but because they're boring. The mature man can't get too excited about a football game—unless he or a member of his family is in it.

WHEN WE START BRINGING LOVE TO OUR GROUPS, MANY OF US FIND NEW GROUPS.

Man unites himself with the world in the process of creation.
—ERIC FROMM

In our isolation, we became anesthetized. It is true that *anesthetized* implies without sensation, "comfortably numb," but in fact the reality of our anesthetized state was more sinister than that. As we accumulated things, to the exclusion of the spirit, we felt expansive and safe but in fact knew we were little and in danger.

Unable to feel, we were unable to create. Unable to create, we were frightened and alone. Here *anesthesia* means, in fact, without aesthetic, this is, as Lewis Hyde puts it, "We were living without the ability to sense *creatively.*" We were always off center because we had lost the knowledge of a center at all. We lacked the ability to know the wholeness of our lives because we could not see the great relatedness within what appeared chaotic.

AS WE TEAR DOWN THE WALLS WE BUILT AND END OUR ISOLATION, WE REGAIN OUR CREATIVITY AND WITH IT, THROUGH COMMUNITY, OUR HOPE AND OUR WHOLENESS.

May 7

Our health is our sound relation to external objects; our sympathy with external beings.
—RALPH WALDO EMERSON

Men in transition from the old patterns of Warrior and Lord to the life of Lover and Mate will open ancient wounds and be wounded anew in the process. Such wounding must be healed and the healing must be given time. Most importantly, our healing must begin where we are! If we wish to heal our wounds, not cauterize them, we must learn to touch our world gently and to hear with our hearts. We must learn, as well, to heal our wounds, not to blame those who we feel wounded us. If you are shot in the ass with an arrow, you don't yell at the archer, you remove the arrow.

LOOKING DEEPLY, I CAN SEE THE WOUNDS OF THOSE WHO WOUNDED ME.

My initiators are always a part of me. Remaining mindful of them, I honor them and recall my story.

WRITE A LETTER TO YOUR FIRST SEXUAL PARTNER.
MAILING IT IS OPTIONAL.

May 9

There is more to life than increasing its speed.
—MAHATMA GANDHI

Picture a parking lot that serves some large entity—a mall, corporate offices, or an airport, for example. In your mind's eye, notice the parking patterns. Is there even one car left a significant distance from the entrance to the buildings? Did any one person not struggle to park as close as possible to that entrance? Not likely. What is the hurry? We are habituated to speed and efficiency without noticing the toll it takes on our spirit. Just using this simple example: in fighting to get the closest parking place, we increase our blood pressure, exercise indiscriminate hostility, and just generally boil our blood a little thinner.

For today, refuse "instant" anything. Inconvenience yourself. Use a pencil or pen rather than a word processor. Walk the greatest distance possible to every destination. Put your watch in a drawer. Count your breaths.

HOW MUCH FULLER IS YOUR LIFE WHEN IT MOVES
AT WALKING SPEED?

A mindful day.

This is a day of mindfulness. What is sought here is not a unique day, standing distinctly apart from all others, but a day when the practice of mindfulness moves into the foreground. Today is a day of enrichment and heightened awareness. Please bring this wonderful practice into every day.

Mindfulness is not an esoteric practice. Being mindful simply means being awake. For men, being mindful can mean the beginning of the end of the social masculine trance and the dismembered life. In mindfulness we become aware of the fullness and flow of our lives, one moment at a time.

The Appendix of this book contains specific directions and suggestions. I encourage you to visit a library or bookstore for additional help in this ancient practice. One excellent book is *Full Catastrophe Living* by Jon Kabat-Zinn, Ph.D. The Vietnamese Buddhist monk Thich Naht Hahn has written dozens of books, many of which concern mindfulness. My personal favorites are *The Miracle of Mindfulness* and *Being Peace*.

This is a beautiful day. Please embrace if fully.

May 11

What do we do when it is not war that is killing us,
but progress?
—ELIZABETH ROBERTS *and* ELIAS AMIDON

There are no enemies left to blame. There is not an other we can point to as the villain who has enraptured our spirits with bells and whistles.

Men have been entranced by speed and progress from childhood, and now we are in grave danger of creating the same trance for our children. It is painful to confront the responsibility for what has become of our spirits and the spirits outside of us. It pushes against a fragile tissue separating who we think we are from who we are. We fear that if that tissue rips, our lives will be lost when in fact all that will be lost is our killing.

WE MEN ARE BEGINNING TO REMEMBER WHO WE ARE.
AS WE AWAKEN WE ARE RECLAIMING OUR AWE AND WONDER.
AS WE ACCEPT WHAT WE BECAME,
WE EMBRACE WHAT WE ARE BECOMING.

May 12

The whole mechanism of modern life is geared for a flight from God and from the spirit into the wilderness of neurosis.
—THOMAS MERTON

Our minds have been filled with fantasies of sex, money, and power; at quiet moments we relived erotic embraces that never happened, or imagined the grand lives we would live, very soon, when things changed a bit; perhaps we congratulated ourselves on our great material achievements. Some of us went further yet and became quite pleased with our spiritual attainments. "You may drive a big Cadillac, but I got God sitting next to me." Sitting alone, in quiet, was a frightening prospect for many men. We would do anything at all to avoid mindful solitude.

Ironically, we isolated ourselves to avoid being alone. Without community, that is, without God and the spirit, we were quietly neurotic and chronically displeased with our state.

Now we are beginning to disable the machine that supported us in our desperate apartness. We are creating a community of stories and shared effort, and are finding our way back home.

WHEN I AM RUNNING AWAY, THERE I AM. WHEN I AM STILL, WHERE AM I?

May 13

The object of all the ceremonies is to bring down the spirits from above, even their ancestors.
—Li Chi
Book of Rites

Have our ceremonies served us well? Ceremonies, secular or religious, pass unnoticed in most cases. The repetition over time strips even the most sacred of ceremonies of any meaning. Further, they have been bled of significance by an unspoken consensus of officials and participants.

Men, in a time of the renewal of manhood, are experiencing a renewal of ceremony. This need is deeply felt and sometimes foolishly expressed. We have the right to appear foolish. In my men's group we ring bells, chant our own poems, and hold hands and pray together. There is another consensus at work here, a heartening one that says to enter into this ceremony with faith but without hope. Our primary prayer is no longer "my will be done." In our ceremonies, we are affirming our humility and our gratitude. Our spirits rise and touch the spirits of our ancestors and of those who will succeed us. Ceremonies, even the most solitary, are never performed alone.

WHAT MUNDANE ACT, SEEN DEEPLY, IS A CEREMONY? HOW CAN IT BE CELEBRATED?

I am living my own myth, not someone else's, no matter how interesting or dramatic. Mindful of my story, I can sense the direction of my life.

CHOOSE A TITLE FOR YOUR AUTOBIOGRAPHY.

May 15

*Eat and carouse with Bacchus, or munch dry bread with Jesus,
but don't sit down without one of the gods.*
—D.H. LAWRENCE

On the night that the Gulf War began, my wife and stepchildren and I prayed together for the first time. We held hands and prayed for the safety of children and of warriors. We prayed for the knowledge that we were safe in an unsafe world.

It was difficult and embarrassing for us to pray together. The adults were long out of the habit of family prayer and for the children, it was too new and too strange. Weren't they supposed to be fighting for supremacy over the serving platters?

Since then we have rarely sat down "without one of the gods." It has been hard to overcome the fear and the embarrassment, but now even the smallest child notices if we forget to pray at mealtime and, I suspect, the older children pray at bedtime as well.

HOW CAN I BE AWARE OF SPIRIT IN MY RITUALS?

May 16

Healing may not be so much about getting better, as about letting go of everything that isn't you—all of the expectations, all of the beliefs—and becoming who you are.
—RACHEL NAOMI REMEN

I was not born with my beliefs or my ideas. The expectations—that I be a "real man," a warrior, a professional success, a landowner, and a whiz at poker—may have gotten under my skin, but they are not my skin.

In renewal, I have the task of ripping out all the bits and pieces that were stuck on, willy-nilly, and revealing the wholeness beneath. I do not lose anything in this process. Rather, I regain that which was lost or amputated by the great artifice I built up over time.

YOU CAN'T GET IT TOGETHER WITHOUT TAKING IT APART.

May 17

Love is the most universal, the most tremendous and the most mysterious of the cosmic forces. After centuries of tentative effort, social institutions have externally diked and canalized it.
—PIERRE TEILHARD DE CHARDIN

We have tried, successfully we tell ourselves, to insure that love does not invade our business or political lives. In fact, of course, we have failed and in that failure have severed these institutions from a source of true power. Men, and more recently women, have for years spent many of their most fruitful and creative hours in "loveless" environments. What we are beginning to see now is that the love was there, underground, and was simply denied. Profit was not likely to soar in an environment where the spirit soared as well. Practicing the politics of exclusion would scrape at the soul of the most hardened man if he allowed himself to see the hearts of those on the outside of his circle.

As men face the task of renewal, the force of love cannot be denied—it is what is motivating it. Long supressed, the power has spread and deepened. As our friends and mates begin to feel the opening of their hearts, each of us can identify with that tightness in the chest and the feeling as it begins to loosen.

WHERE IS IT THAT LOVE DOES NOT BELONG?

May 18

The neatly knotted tie is all that's left of our desert shawl and shaman robe.
—MICHAEL VENTURA

One of the worst pieces of advice I ever read was for men to wear brightly colored underwear with conservative business clothes. Isn't there something just a little tepid about that? Actions such as that dishonor our work and ourselves. What's the secret we're supposed to hide? That we are not comfortable bringing our dicks to work? "Sorry, I left it in my Levi's." The role of the shaman, in his multicolored robes and feathers, is certainly not for every man. But we are no longer sure that the role of business acolyte, in grays and blues and power ties, fits us all terribly well either.

We are learning to be wholly who we are, at our desks and at our dinner tables. This is not an easy journey; early on, this path shows us how much we have put on to cover up who we were, and that additional subterfuge further diminishes our awakening.

DON'T WEAR UNDERPANTS AT ALL. TRY THAT TODAY IF YOU WANT TO FEEL LIBERATED—OR FOOLISH.

May 19

Unable to serve as plants, we must serve as manure.
—EDWARD CONZE

Take a closer look at the plants today. Think like the grass or flowers. Imagine the work they do, just getting where they are. Examine a blade of grass. What colors do you see there? How did that happen?

Who helped?

Do you still think of yourself as special or separate?

Can you think of yourself as plant food?

MY PLACE IS IN THE LARGER WORLD.

May 20

We have forgotten who we are.
We ask forgiveness
We ask for the gift of remembering
We ask for the strength to change.
We have forgotten who we are.
—U.N. ENVIRONMENTAL SABBATH PROGRAM

We have an intuitive awareness of our kinship with all the natural world. It comes to us in undefended moments, as when the *kaaaaaaaa* of the cicada penetrates our bones and sounds within us, unnamed. For modern, civilized, corporate unincorporated man, it is difficult to remain connected to this larger world. We have been suspicious and restless when we felt peace in the presence of flowering plants, tall grasses, or the sinuous flow of wild water. We have rushed up mountains, intent on the goal and missing the journey.

We are awakening to who we are. It is not so different from who we were. We can be born again into our simple rightful home and, in loving it and husbanding it, lift our spirits out of despair and isolation and into harmony with the greater spirit to which we have always been connected.

WAKING UP TODAY, I VOW TO WAKE UP.

May 21

What am I doing, saying "foxtail pine"?
—GARY SNYDER

As we reclaim our home in the natural world, or better, as we ask for forgiveness and make amends to the natural world, and humbly ask to be reinstated in our small niche, we need to understand that we don't understand it very well. Men, the assigned warriors, made war against nature on behalf of an unenlightened patriarchy and in order to make war (called "taming the wilderness" or "developing resources") we had to make it all make sense. When, as George Bush once said, "the Earth spoke back," we were not prepared for the power of that voice. We acted as if we were outside of nature or acted out of the belief in dominion with its suggestion of the right to control.

We are renewing our knowledge of kinship now. The earth is forever altered by the days of our isolation and so are we—men, women, all creatures. Spring will be different this year from any spring of our boyhood. How will it be different? What difference can a man make this spring?

CAN I VOW THAT SPRINGTIMES TO COME,
FOR SEVEN GENERATIONS, WILL MARK THE GROWING HEALTH
OF OUR PLANET?

Mindful of my relation to all things, I must consider the myth of my uniqueness and separation. I can consider where I began and where I will end and see my connectedness.

WHERE DID YOU COME FROM? METAPHYSICS ARE NOT OPTIONAL.
(THANKS TO SAM KEEN FOR THIS ONE.)

May 23

If there ever was a sign of hope, it is that single blade of
grass splitting through concrete.
Brave Old World!
—JOEL MONTURE

Every drop of water in the Esopus River is going to
find its way to the sea, no matter how many dams and res-
ervoirs the state of New York might build. That force is relentless.

Each day we can find reminders of this great power
of nature, but we have learned to overlook it; we have desensitized ourselves to it in order to play out whatever
twisted male story we never told ourselves. Wardens and
healers of the earth, we lost our way from the campfire and
found ourselves, wounded and lonely, in stone canyons,
carrying gadgets and adjusting our neckties, while our
souls longed for wildness.

On this day, the nearby rivers are straining toward
the sea, the grass is crumbling tarmac, the neighborhood
dogs are barking the needs of their bodies.

PAY ATTENTION.

May 24

Gardening is an active participation in the deepest mysteries of the universe.
—THOMAS BERRY

Our push-button lives, with shrill bells and shriller whistles, failed at last. No number of gadgets, promising quicker communication, speedier relief, or greater profit, would fill the empty spaces that we felt. We confused noise and movement with activity. Our daytime lives were a walk through the sideshow and our waking nights were spent in passive pursuits. Dreamtime was denied us and we rarely woke refreshed and grateful, feeling the sun or hearing the rain.

Now we are part of a larger reality. We are actively involved with life; no longer content to watch what others have cooked up for us we plant our own flowers or take hikes in the parks, slowly, looking for the messages in the bushes just off to the side of the path. Some men grow their own vegetables and watch with close attention as the flowers they planted begin to grow in springtime.

We are learning to feel gratitude as we are allowed to be part of the natural process. We recognize that the spiritual masculine is active and we rejoice in that knowledge.

I AM PART OF, NOT APART FROM, THE NATURAL RHYTHMS WITH THEIR WONDER AND THEIR TERROR.

May 25

Cultivate your garden. Let it take root in you until your thousand eyes open like violets to morning light.
—NANCY PADDOCK

The stifling of imagination is a great wound and one that requires much effort to heal. We remember our boyhoods when we could see the most remarkable creatures and structures in places where others saw only rocks, furniture, clumps of trees, or empty sky. We could easily imagine our thousand eyes flashing open and startling the whole universe. Light came from our fingertips and waves of energy poured from the knife edges of our small hands, waving about in the sweet air.

That delicious gift is not gone. We can spend some time each day reclaiming it. It's best to be cautious and not fall into the trap of "using" the gift in work, for example. Imagination certainly fits there but not only there. Here we are dealing with frivolous and random flights of great childlike inventiveness. Today we can see the critter peering around the corner or the ghostly flotilla on Fifth Avenue.

TODAY A ROSE CAN BLOOM IN MY OPENING FIST.

I observe myself and so I come to know others.
—LAO-TSE

Our understanding is shaped by our looking and our seeing. We can't hope to find the inner joys of our lives with our vision restricted or unfocused. Prejudice and intolerance affect where we put our eyes, as do fear and shame. We wouldn't look into the eyes of homeless men and women, but at their rags. We looked away from the sadness of our children and of the children of the greater community. We looked at our families and saw only the hurting but never the pain.

When we put our eyes on the beauty, it reflects in us. When we put our eyes on the sorrow, we are moved to relieve it. Here is a great secret that men are understanding now: looking doesn't hurt, it heals.

HEY, WHAT ARE YOU LOOKING AT?

May 27

Poetry is adolescence fermented and thus preserved.
　　　　　　　　　　　　　　—Jose Ortega y Gasset

Write a poem. Don't buy a book on how to write a poem. Write a poem. Today is the day to watch the imagination take off, shaking flakes of carapace to the downdraft.

James Lee Burke said in an interview that his books were already written before he got to them; he just had to let them come through. Today's poem is in you, held tightly to the heart of a fifteen-year-old filled with hope and scattered wonder. Let him speak.

Looking deeply, I will release a poem today.

May 28

America, I'm putting my queer shoulder to the wheel.
—ALLEN GINSBERG

Where are the boundaries of our kinship? Will Allen Ginsberg put his queer shoulder next to my straight one to turn the wheel? Will I get next to him in the work that must be done? Will I stand, shoulder to shoulder, with Gloria or Letty, to get the work done?

The journey toward wholeness and home includes dismantling barriers we've built along the way. The "others" I have fenced out have successfully fenced me in. . . .

WHO IS IT THAT I EXCLUDE? CAN I LOOK AT WHY I DO IT?

May 29

. . . (the prerequisite) of maturity consist(s) first in the breaking down of the small "I"—that is to say, the "I" that rejects pain, is full of fears, and is solely concerned with the things of the world.

—KARLFRIED GRAF DURCKHEIM

We have not matured well, many of us. The work was too great and the charts had disappeared. We lost our way. Without guidance and conscious ritual we slipped into prolonged adolescence. The women didn't understand what had happened to us, couldn't make sense of our blighted boyishness. When we allowed ourselves to press the vulnerable spots, we were bewildered by the unnameable pain we felt. We limited our lives to avoid what we feared, but it would not leave us alone. Bats fly in the daytime as well, so hiding at night was futile. When the pains of loss came, we built a carapace of indifference or of addictions. We deteriorated and became ill. There was no inner life to strengthen us.

Then the day came, through a phone call, a trip to a bookstore, a visit with a friend, when we saw that there was a way out of our toxic childhood. We stepped into the void and found a footbridge.

Surrounded by the world, we looked inside and found the strength that all the things of the world could not give us. We also see, for the first time perhaps, that the world does offer great gifts we had not seen.

I HAVE BEGUN TO SEE THAT THE GREATEST GIFTS OF THE WORLD
ARE ITS TASKS RATHER THAN ITS THINGS.

May 30

It is no ordinary thing simply to say to Thee, O God, thank you so much, thank you so very much, our Father.
—HOWARD THURMAN

Prayer erupts out of us, in unguarded times, free of made-up language and tortured self-consciousness. Will God like my prayer? What God? Is he within me or out there? Is he a she? We can go on endlessly in the debates with our critical minds, trying to get it right the way we were taught or trying to get it right in vigorous opposition to the way we were taught. And in the meantime "Hallelujah" is stuck in our throats.

The spirited male is likely to shout out his gratitude and his joy in the most unlikely places. He can't be trusted not to laugh during the sermon or not to look upward, eyes open, while he leads his family in a spontaneous prayer of thanksgiving for the take-out pizza.

The masculine spirit is active, expressive, joyous, and persistent. Spontaneity, once feared or mimed, marks many of our days. Say Hallelujah!

TODAY I CAN BE DANGEROUS;
I CAN SHOUT A PRAYER IN THE STREET.

May 31

A mindful day.

This is a day of mindfulness. What is sought here is not a unique day, standing distinctly apart from all others, but a day when the practice of mindfulness moves into the foreground. Today is a day of enrichment and heightened awareness. Please bring this wonderful practice into every day.

Mindfulness is not an esoteric practice. Being mindful simply means being awake. For men, being mindful can mean the beginning of the end of the social masculine trance and the dismembered life. In mindfulness we become aware of the fullness and flow of our lives, one moment at a time.

The Appendix of this book contains specific directions and suggestions. I encourage you to visit a library or bookstore for additional help in this ancient practice. One excellent book is *Full Catastrophe Living* by Jon Kabat-Zinn, Ph.D. The Vietnamese Buddhist monk Thich Naht Hahn has written dozens of books, many of which concern mindfulness. My personal favorites are *The Miracle of Mindfulness* and *Being Peace*.

This is a beautiful day. Please embrace it fully.

June 1

In Greek mythology, the seventeenth of June marks the marriage of Orpheus and Eurydice. We can glorify the ancient ritual of marriage during this month, feeling the power of this commitment to the "sacred ordeal" of matrimony.

Also observed this month are Inti Raymi, the Inca sun festival; Rath Yatra, the Hindu festival of the Lord; and Hajj, the first day of pilgrimage to Mecca in Islam.

June 2

Fear that our thoughts are poisonous and best kept quietly under wraps has kept many of us from feeling satisfaction or partnership with other men. We felt so driven to be admired by men that we tried to do what the culture told us made us male. We slept with as many women as we could, keeping count and filing away anecdotes to be retold in the company of men. We became fathers, often making these babies proof of our virility rather than evidence of a great power before which we stand humbled.

In the discovery and renewal of our mature masculinity, many of us, through story-telling or close talk with another man, have uncovered deep affinities that we never expected. We have found that other men are uncertain of their ability to father well enough, or that they too find it far more difficult to turn to their partner for erotic discovery than to "bang," with all those overtones of violence, a stranger.

I AM NOT ALONE. THE UNDEFENDED SPIRIT IS SAFE IN THE COMPANY OF OTHER MEN, AND WILL FIND HOME AND WHOLENESS.

June 3

... a man who fails to pursue self-knowledge is and remains a danger to society, for he will tend to misunderstand everything that other people say or do, and remain blissfully unaware of the significance of many of the things he does himself.
—E.F. SCHUMACHER

We have been entranced and disembodied; habituated to consuming and discarding. Wounded ourselves, we have wounded others in our enchantment with people, places, and things.

It has become difficult not to see the results of our past actions; our charades of indifference and buckpassing have crumbled. No one is fooled. Yet we feared the end of our trance. It was comforting. We avoided pain and rationalized our fears. But we knew, in a deep and hidden place, that we were not men, but boys, and the pain of that secret knowledge finally became too much to bear.

The Lover/man is happily disenchanted. He has begun the journey within and, not avoiding pain or giving in to fear, has seen the faint outlines of his greater self. In being healed, he becomes a healer. As a true lover, he looks inside himself and sees into distant generations and knows the effects of his actions today on those who will come long after him, and he cares about them.

We have traveled in the dark for a long time. Yet we could blossom even there, with faith in the light to come.

I WILL NOT PERISH IN SELF-EXAMINATION.

June 4

Becoming mindful of the surroundings I have made and the things I have accumulated, I see an accurate picture of myself.

LOOK AT THE BOOKS YOU OWN. WRITE AN BRIEF
AUTOBIOGRAPHICAL SKETCH BASED ON WHAT YOU FIND.
(I OWN THREE COPIES OF CHOGYAM TRUNGPA'S
CUTTING THROUGH SPIRITUAL MATERIALISM.
I THINK THAT'S A PROBLEM.)

*When the Earth is sick and polluted, human health is impossi-
ble. . . . To heal ourselves we must heal our planet and to heal our
planet we must heal ourselves.*
—BOBBY McLEOD

We make the air we breathe and the air we breathe is
killing us and is reweaving DNA, a strand at a time, caus-
ing grotesque mutations that we have yet to encounter. We
have "conquered" nature—the Columbia River, for
example—and have destroyed whole species, whole species upon whose survival our own survival rests.

Men, traditionally, are not stewards of the earth, but
its codependent protectors. Our renewed masculine energy,
the masculine spirit, is rushing toward the bruises and
wounds of decades of warring with our homes. We are
finding we are incapable of truly healing the planet without healing ourselves, passively and actively. As we experience our codependence with this earth through our healing
process, we are compelled to honor our home. As we
honor our home, it blesses us with health and spiritual
vigor.

Each day, we can look more closely at our habits and
see how they effect our home and, amending them, heal
some small part of our environment and thus heal ourselves.

THE WELL-BEING OF ALL CREATION RESTS ON MY WELL-BEING.
THEY ARE NOT SEPARATE.

June 6

They have blessed each other, the ultimate gift,
the deepest healing.
—BILL MOYERS

Men are beginning to give to their mates, their children, and their friends gifts far greater than they have been accustomed to giving. We are giving our true attention, our care, and our blessings.

In the past, we have dumped only things, nearly numberless and quickly forgotten, on those close to us rather than giving the gift of ourselves. Unaccustomed to feeling, we were threatened by the feelings of others and so withdrew. Benumbed and disenfranchised by the demands of orthodox religion, we could not be touched by the spiritual needs of those we wished to love.

Now that we have become willingly unprotected, we find that we have great resources of strength, courage, and serenity. Guided by a desire to live usefully, we can give of ourselves and in doing that we offer our blessings.

🌳 🌳 🌳

THE BLESSINGS WE OFFER TODAY ARE THE HEALING GIFTS OF AN
INCARNATE SPIRIT AND A GRATEFUL HEART.

June 7

Why should we consider prayer an embarrassing exception to the rule that imagination, fantasy, personification, analogy, and dramatization are invaluable techniques for positioning ourselves creatively in the world?
—SAM KEEN

Elsewhere, prayer has been defined as creative mumbling. It is not an exercise that comes easily to most men. It is particularly unlikely that you will find the former president of Sigma Gotcha, now a Very Important Executive in the Cosmodemonic Telegraph Company (with a tip of the hat to H. Miller), on his unclad knees, morning and night, joining, in his isolated act, with children across his town and country, in the act of thanking some unseen other for that which he vainly hopes he has achieved all on his own.

Men pray. Just as men work, play, make love, and tussle with their children, they pray. Men pray just as they suffer, grieve, hope, and are anxious or uncertain. Many of us are discovering that the habit of some acknowledgment of a power greater than ourselves brings comfort, hope, and humility in a world that does not see these qualities right-sized.

Men pray. On their knees or walking down the street, at regular times or at odd hours, alone or in groups or a combination of the two. Men pray and they mean what they say.

I AM MAN ENOUGH TO GET ON MY KNEES.

June 8

To live consciously is to move through life with conscious self-remembering.
—DUANE ELGIN

Much of the task of masculine renewal is to reclaim our own lives, to discard the roles we accepted thoughtlessly, which have caused such distress to ourselves and our world. We are involved in remembering ourselves, becoming whole, that is. As we become conscious of ourselves in our lives, at every moment, we begin to live more voluntarily, Elgin points out. Voluntary living is living without so many blind habits and needs. Living this way destroys the illusions of need which cause us such pain in the long run and which, wounding us, wound our families, our communities, and our habitat. Living consciously and voluntarily enables us to appreciate the simpler acts and gifts of our "ordinary" lives and in the process the ordinary becomes extraordinary. For example, a deep breath, consciously taken in the midst of a hectic day, draws all of the universe into our bodies. We sparkle with energy, and what was hectic becomes calm.

Today can be a day of conscious living. As you have read these words, have you been aware of yourself reading them? Or have you been lost? Read them again, remaining conscious of yourself reading them. That is an exercise in conscious living. Where else will that feeling fit in your day?

🌱 🌱 🌱

ARE YOU DIZZY?

June 9

The little things? The little moments? They aren't little.
—JON KABAT-ZINN

We have become so accustomed to racing about, getting what we think we need and keeping away from what we think we don't need, that we miss what we have. We eat without tasting, make love without feeling, and work without passion. The sunrise is without color and the day passes in streams of gray. A conversation with a friend is attended with half a mind, while the rest is fragmented by parking meters, checkbooks, meetings to come, and meetings past. We often end a day heartsick and weary-minded, and can only think to "entertain" ourselves to relieve the anxiety, all the time a little suspicious that this too is shredding our aliveness.

Living voluntarily, we begin to put all the great rush and anxiety behind us. We can practice seeing the morning and tasting our food. Conversations can go on and on, deeper and broader, as we learn to explore the nuances of our life process. We can go into a room without turning on the radio or TV. We can sit with a quiet mind and feel the breezes. Thus enriched, we begin to learn the practice of gratitude for the great expanse of life, now noticed in its details.

WHAT'S THE RUSH?

June 10

Becoming mindful of the people and places of my life and reflecting deeply on them, I grow in power and humility.

FIND, ON A MAP, THE PLACE WHERE YOUR PATERNAL GRANDMOTHER WAS BORN.

June 11

Man's loneliness is but his fear of life.
—EUGENE O'NEILL

Our dis-ease is the illusion of loneliness and isolation. We struggle to get along, to get through, to get a break. We have learned to sentimentalize and romanticize this illusion of separateness; to make a virtue of our pain in order to deny it. When I was (much) younger, my anthem was Vince Martins's song, "I'm a Drifter, I'm a Loner."

Once we fall into reality, we are, at that moment, connected to all of life. The rest of the process is in recognizing that simple fact. The "religious" man is the man who knows, in his deepest self, that he is connected to the source of his being at every moment. The men who go to church may or may not be religious. The same is true of men who never go to church, who never formally pray, who do not "believe" in God.

A religious man is a man who cannot be lonely and who is not afraid of life.

🌳 🌳 🌳

TODAY I WILL LOOK DEEPLY AT MY FEAR.

June 12

If any man obeys the gods, they listen to him also.
—HOMER

When Carl Jung was asked if he believed in God, he replied that he did not; rather, he *knew* God. This experience of union with God seems a time-swallowing and difficult task to most men, one hardly worth the effort. But as we have looked deeper into the questions, we have seen how central they have been for us, and how many different and futile answers we have found. We have danced our lives in front of women, seeking approval. We have found spirit in spirits and drugs or in money and things. Our corporations have replaced the Sunday schools of childhood. The questions persisted and the thirst for spirit grew.

As we have thrown out the final barriers, the barriers of "I can't," or "it's not men's work," or "that's for the rabbi or priest to tell me once a week," or "I don't believe," we have felt more immediately the need for knowledge of a power greater than ourselves.

The poets and the mystics tell us that to seek God is to know God. We are open to that reality now. Through men's groups, or through recommitment to our childhood faith, through involvement in community at deeper and profoundly different levels, or through true friendship with our partners, we are discovering spiritual power at the tips of our fingers.

❦ ❦ ❦

WHAT IS THE PATH TO GOD FOR ME TODAY?

June 13

The great man is he who does not lose his child's heart.
—MENCIUS

It is necessary to tread cautiously here. There are few people more vain and foolish than a grown man still trying to perfect the moods and the rhythms of his boyhood. Childhood ends, but the heart of the child pounds on, delighting, awkward, trusting, loving, and open. The heart of the child takes delight in the wonder of a single toy; the childish man only accumulates trophy toys. The child's heart is warm; the heart of a childish man is cold. The wholehearted child inspires joy; the childish man is uninspiring.

🌿 🌿 🌿

THE MAN IN FULL AND CONSCIOUS POSSESSION OF HIS CHILD'S HEART IS WHOLE. HIS LIFE IS USEFUL AND HIS DESIRES ARE FEW.

June 14

A mindful day.

This is a day of mindfulness. What is sought here is not a unique day, standing distinctly apart from all others, but a day when the practice of mindfulness moves into the foreground. Today is a day of enrichment and heightened awareness. Please bring this wonderful practice into every day.

Mindfulness is not an esoteric practice. Being mindful simply means being awake. For men, being mindful can mean the beginning of the end of the social masculine trance and the dismembered life. In mindfulness we become aware of the fullness and flow of our lives, one moment at a time.

The Appendix of this book contains specific directions and suggestions. I encourage you to visit a library or bookstore for additional help in this ancient practice. One excellent book is *Full Catastrophe Living* by Jon Kabat-Zinn, Ph.D. The Vietnamese Buddhist monk Thich Naht Hahn has written dozens of books, many of which concern mindfulness. My personal favorites are *The Miracle of Mindfulness* and *Being Peace*.

This is a beautiful day. Please embrace it fully.

June 15

I hate and love.
You ask, perhaps, how that can be?/
I know not, but I feel the agony.
—CATULLUS

Our bodies often know what our minds can't understand. Caught in the spiral downward, the body is heavy and unmanageable; unrestful sleep commands us into oblivion. We descend into the underworld several times in our lives, corpulent with dread. In years past, men would deny the descent, feelings cauterized by addictions. The energy of ascent would remain frozen in our bodies.

Now we understand that halting the descent denies us the freedom of the ascent toward the light. The trip downward prepares the upward path. In times of distress, we can allow ourselves to share our fears and our anger with others. In the time of light, we are able therefore to share our experience.

I WILL READ DEEPLY THE MESSAGES FROM MY BODY.

June 16

We have to treat others as part of who we are, rather than as a "them" with whom we are in constant competition.
—ROBERT BELLAH

We were taught to say "there but for the Grace of God go I." We are learning to say, simply, "There go I."

Many men are sickened by the corruption and trivilialization of our society and by the destruction of our planet. This is the home of our children's children, down to seven generations and beyond. We don't like to see it Disneyfied, corporatized, and leveled for parking lots.

But we are also sickened by our own anger.

Now we are practicing connection rather than competition; we are trying to see that there is no "enemy," no "them" to blame. As we see what a mess we have become, we can no longer sit in judgment on others.

What men are learning now is to heal themselves and, concurrently, to experience the cohealing of the earth and the people. The longer we work at living voluntarily, the better the people around us get. The harder we work at living mindfully, the healthier the planet gets. The deeper we look within, the further we can see beyond.

TODAY I WILL PRACTICE SAYING "THERE GO I" AND FEEL THE WALLS GO DOWN.

June 17

Considering mindfully how I am made up of many elements, I can see a future I couldn't consider when I lived in the illusion of separation.

<small>WHERE WILL YOU BE 200 YEARS FROM NOW?</small>

June 18

> *By compassion, we make others' misery our own and so,*
> *by relieving them, we relieve ourselves also.*
> —SIR THOMAS BROWNE

To be compassionate means, literally, to "suffer with." As a man becomes more sensitized to his real environment and begins to live in his body and his feelings, rather than in his head, he begins to suffer in unfamiliar ways. He can no longer share in a sense of "victory" when tens of thousands are killed in a war. He weeps with the trees of the rain forest as they "weep their sap after the fire," as Marion Woodman says. He can no longer tell his son that "big boys don't cry" because he knows that they do.

When I told my son Willie, at age three, that I cried sometimes and felt sad, he said, "But you shouldn't do it alone. You need to find somebody." In that moment, Willie won the basketball game in the final seconds, climbed Mount Analogue, protested a war with his body, and gave life to his children, all tied up in one sweet and heartfelt statement.

SUFFERING WITH OTHERS, SUFFERING WITH THE WORLD, WE CAN
PUT AN END TO SUFFERING.

Don't apologize for the sorrow, grief and rage you feel. It is a measure of your humanity and your maturity.
—JOANNA MACY

We live in a "psychologized" age. If we are concerned about abused children, the pundits say that we are working out the issues of our unclaimed inner child. When we are horrified by the collapse of the eco-structure and the filth poured into our air and water, it is suggested that we are anal and perhaps overly prissy. The list of pop-psych descriptions of our unconscious conflicts goes on forever; psychologized man frets about why he reacts so to these (very real) crises, and nothing gets done.

At one point, my publisher wanted to call this book a guide to "stress-free living." I suggested that the person who made that suggestion should read the book first. Wanting to live without stress is part of the problem—an extension of the adolescent, self-preoccupied "man-ness" that has caused such catastrophes as this bloody century has seen.

It is natural and it is right for a man to feel this sorrow, grief, and rage. If we don't feel stressed, we are missing big pieces of our lives. This is the reality of spirited men. We are no longer willing to infantilize ourselves and our powerful spiritual reactions to the sickness of the world. We are learning that our souls are crying, not our neuroses, and we are taking action, led by our intuition, compassion, and strengths.

WHEN I FEEL UPSET TODAY, I WILL LOOK CLOSELY.
PERHAPS SOMETHING NEEDS DOING.

June 20

We have been "endarkened" as men, led by the patriarchal corporatized culture to overwork, overplay, overdo, and overcompensate. In the process, our hearts have been attacked or broken, we have drifted softly into alcoholism, drug addiction, incoherent rage, or suffocating depression. Often, too, we have been carried into this special hell wrapped in silk and velvet, all too willing to surrender our spirits.

At the last moment, we awoke. We went from a world where we would wryly smile, shrug our tight shoulders, and say "shit happens" to a new world where, as the shadows yield to light, we are learning that Grace happens. We have been carried by Grace to a new way of seeing and caring. We are confident that on the perilous road home, we can live in Grace.

We also know that the awareness of Grace is a gift that must be acknowledged daily and grows when shared. We're not alone anymore; we are awake and going home, gracefully.

Ψ Ψ Ψ

GRACE HAPPENS!

Religion is for people who are afraid of hell. The spiritual life is for those who have been there.
—ANONYMOUS

Hell is the place of greed, anger, and ignorance. It is the domain of the disconnected, isolated self. Our fascination with the autistic or schizophrenic child is a fascination with hell's meanest rooms. In hell, people are objects. We count the number of women or men we have balled. When a child is hurt by a teacher or coach, we wonder, at once, what the child did to deserve it. In hell, we celebrate war.

When men began talking with each other, listening with the heart, the doors out of hell were opened. As we continue to conspire, that is, to "breathe together," the doors open wider. We tell our stories and in telling them, begin to understand where we have been and where we can go. We listen, openly, to our partners, mates, parents, children, and all of our teachers, sentient and insentient. We cease to be at odds with the world and begin to see our place in it and then know what the tasks of the heart are.

WHERE IN HELL AM I?

June 22

By becoming mindful of my influence, I deepen my ability to love humbly and powerfully.

June 23

When I was a child, I spake as a child, I understood as a child, I thought as a child: but when I became a man, I put away childish things.
—1 Corinthians 13:11

It is hard to be a "grown-up" when the markers are so puzzling. Are we grown-up when we have certain things, or when we have passed a certain age? Is a grown-up a man, over forty, with a wife, a job, children, and a nice car? When we grow pubic hair, when our voices move into our chests and when we have fought a war, are we men then?

Perhaps we have become men when we think it is more important to be soft than to be hard.

The Convent Men's Group defines a man as one who has converted experience into wisdom and who willingly acts from and shares that achieved wisdom.

❦ ❦ ❦

What does this word man mean to me?

June 24

In a man's middle years there is scarcely a part of the body he would hesitate to turn over to the proper authorities.
—E.B. W‍HITE

At this writing, I am a half century old and it's just tinker, tinker, tinker. What goes down doesn't always come up, I've had three episodes of skin cancer, ten teeth have been yanked out of my mouth, several bones were removed from my toes, my knees hurt most of the time, my eyes are no good, and my chest is trying to go south. I'm beginning to wonder if I'm interested in the spiritual life solely because I have lost capacity in all the others.

Don't believe it. If you're there already, you know, as Logan Pearsall Smith said, "There is more felicity on the far side of baldness than young men can possibly imagine." If you are not, you suspect Smith and me to be fools.

Here is what else is so about me. I practice Aikido, run several miles nearly every day, have a rich erotic life, play basketball with my children, cook the family's meals, know who my friends are, and am deeply involved in a spiritual practice that leads effortlessly into responsible community action.

A‍SK YOURSELF HOW OLD YOU REALLY ARE.

*I should like to enjoy this summer flower by flower, as if it were
to be the last one for me.*
—ANDRÉ GIDE

The practice of mindful living opens our environment to us and exposes wonders we never imagined during the years we spent entranced. There is a holiness and
fullness to our days now; the present is a good place to be.
We are less concerned about the future and as we live more
in the here and now, the future simply pours in to the present, unnamed.

TODAY I WILL KNOW THAT MY FEET ARE FIRMLY PLANTED.

June 26

We are healed of a suffering only by experiencing it to the full.
—MARCEL PROUST

No one is exempt. No one can see around the corner. No one can escape. Some event, some sudden unseen truth, some "simple twist of fate" brings each of us face-to-face with our own private horror. Some break; some see the other side.

It is at these times that our resources, inner and outer, are pushed beyond foreseeable limits. It is at these times of hitting bottom that we are given a test we can rarely endure alone.

It is here that many men have the direct experience of a power greater than themselves. Patient angels appear from darkened corners of the mourner's room. Prayers, screamed from the heart, are answered in miracles of the heart.

GOD ENTERS THROUGH THE WOUND.

June 27

This much is certain: it is easier to get through a lifetime with an intact spirit by learning the art of repentance and forgiveness than by avoiding risks and mistakes.
—SAM KEEN

Men take risks in the work world; speculating in the stock market, asking for a raise, playing office politics, flirting. These, flirting excepted perhaps, are manageable risks with control over outcomes. Some also take physical risks, some spirited, some stupid; climbing mountains, playing football, driving drunk, starting fights.

Now there are greater and more worrisome risks for men to take. There is, first, the risk of discovering one's manhood, unmasking the spirited masculine and setting him on his precarious way home. Mistakes will be made and repentance will be required. It is sometimes difficult for a man to say "I was wrong," but it is harder yet, on the spirit, never to acknowledge one's failures.

We can risk it all, body, mind, and heart, and keep it, or we can refrain from the risk, and lose it.

WHAT IS EASIER FOR ME—TO SAY I WAS WRONG
OR TO AVOID MISTAKES?

June 28

Not I—not anyone else can travel that road for you,
You must travel it for yourself.
—WALT WHITMAN

The journey is to the center of the heart. There we find our original home. The labyrinth we encounter is dammed with our fears, our resistance, our unacknowledged learning. At each turn we face walls only we could have built and that only we can dismantle.

We are served by the experience of other men who have made their voyage, but the true teachers among them will make clear that his voyage is his only. The teacher can show the student what he has done, but is compelled by compassion to let the student go his own way. We are not without help, yet we are totally alone.

The true gift from the teacher is not a road map, but hope. They are witnesses to the end of exile. We see that they are men of power and wisdom, connected to the source. We also know they are human, that they rage and bluster and fuck up the simplest of things. This is another gift—perfection is no longer our goal—and we are pointed headfirst at reality.

WE MAKE THE JOURNEY FROM EXILE ALONE, TRUSTING THAT THE PASSION TO MAKE THE JOURNEY CONTAINS BOTH THE PROOF OF ITS AUTHENTICITY AND THE POWER OF ITS DESTINATION.

June 29

Suzki said: "Childlikeness" has to be restored with long years of training in the art of self-forgetfulness.
—EUGEN HERRIGEL

Take an hour and watch children "at life." You will see spontaneity, trust, awe, great curiosity, puzzlement, true dignity, and delight. You will be seeing you as you were before this complicated adult was constructed.

We wrapped that child with costumes and hid his face with masks; self-centered and self-interested in the extreme, we reached a point of oblivious alienation from the sources of love and caring that once flowed openly into and out of us. The childlike qualities were suffocated beneath the accretions from the endless demands of the socialized, sanitized, sterilized male. We found ourselves in exile, and dying.

That is no longer the case. We are in flight from exile now. As we reconnect with the deeper values and pause to listen to the lives of others, familiar to us and unfamiliar, our costumes fall off in tatters, our masks disintegrate, and, involved with the great dance, we forget the dancer.

CHILDREN WILL BE MY TEACHERS TODAY.

June 30

Awakening to my deeper masculinity, I can sense a spiritual connection. I want to strengthen that connection and recognize that doing so requires ongoing attention.

WRITE A LETTER TO GOD. MAILING IT IS OPTIONAL.

July 1

July fifth is the day the earth is farthest from the sun, the aphelion.

The seventh of this month is Dhamma Day, celebrating the Buddha's first teachings, followed later in the month by Bon, the "Gathering of Joy," a time of celebrating the enlightenment taught by the Buddha.

This is the month of the Muslim new year.

July 2

Superficiality is the curse of our age. The doctrine of instant satisfaction is a primary spiritual problem.
—RICHARD J. FOSTER

Dad comes home from work and has a quick drink to take the edge off. Wide-eyed sons watch the magic work. Mom has a headache and takes an aspirin. Moments later, the headache is gone. It's Easter and the kids want a bunny. Dad proudly buys it, quickly so they'll appreciate it. Or him.

The next day, Dad is on edge again, Mom has that damned headache, and the rabbit, well, it shits too much.

Years later, as grown men, we continued to take spiritual aspirin, feeling the "god-shaped emptiness." We took weekend seminars, or got taken by them. We leapt from pew to bed to meditation cushion to barstool, scarcely stopping to see where we'd been but always certain we knew where we were going. We bit the poisoned apple, went instantly to sleep and began to dream seamless dreams of getting and having.

Now the nightmare is over. We are finding strength and hope in a community of stories. Our commitments have depth and longevity. Our lives are our own.

🌿 🌿 🌿

WHAT IS IT A MAN REALLY NEEDS? CHANCES ARE NOT ONE OF US, ON HIS DEATHBED, WILL WISH HE HAD READ JUST ONE MORE CATALOGUE OR TAKEN ONE MORE SEMINAR.

July 3

*I wanted them [sons Max and Zachary—ed.] to know that their
mom stood for something.*
—MARY FISHER

The children who depend on us know what we stand
for, even if we don't. They see how we spend our time and
our energies, see who our friends are, hear our prejudices,
and see our fears. They see our icons and visit our holy
places with us. They know what we stand for, and they are
never wrong.

Just as our children do, we know, intuitively, what
our mothers and fathers stood for. We are in touch, consciously or unconsciously, with our legacy. It often drives
us as it will drive our children. We need to ask ourselves
what we stand for. We need then to go deeper and ask ourselves if what we say we stand for is realized in action.

Our holy places could be temple, museum, mountains, barroom, or mall. The icons might be automobiles,
crosses, religious art, or fashions. The transformational man
is becoming more at home in silent places than in noisy
ones. His battles are for peace rather than for parking
places. His community is inclusive, not exclusive.

WHAT IS HOLY TO ME? WHERE DO I WORSHIP?

July 4

Better than a thousand useless words is one single word that gives peace.
—THE DHAMMAPADA

A friend who is an analyst once asked me why I was so eager to find a name for the mental illness of someone close to me. Without thinking, I replied, "Because I'm a man. That's what I do." I am not suggesting that to name this problem was improper; in fact, it was valuable in determining the parameters of treatment. I am simply pointing at a tendency I share with many men. I will think, connive, and talk my way through any situation. When a child comes to me in pain, I try to explain away that pain. These are useless words that deny the child's feelings. I am learning now to agree with her that "it hurts" and that it feels like it will never go away.

As best I can, I try to feel the conflict as if it were mine and then ease the pain, offering words of comfort and support, rather than pedagogy and denial.

WHEN SOMEONE ASKS FOR COMFORT,
DO I OFFER MY HEART OR MY ATTITUDE?

We cannot remain consistent with the world save by growing inconsistent with our past selves.
—HAVELOCK ELLIS

    Most men will say that they welcome change, that it's "changing" that's the problem. As we sink more deeply into the rhythms and tempos of the real world, change becomes a part of our lives, rather than a virtue. We must not be so naive as to think that only responding to the natural world is sufficient. There is the world of artifice that demands change and willing inconsistency as well. It is the part of wisdom to see the difference and the part of wisdom in action to put aside those superficial or delusional forces that impede the flow of the truth.

WHAT ARE THE EFFECTS OF MY CONSISTENCY OVER TIME?

July 6

Boys who "will be boys" have little chance of becoming men. We are justifiably horrified when we read of boys who keep a body count of the girls they have had sex with. We can see them as vain and silly oafs whose lives are limited and demeaning. The spirited man recoils at the thought of the heartless narcissism of such children.

So what are you going to do about it?

These horrid boys and their mentors, who seem to pop up like cheap talismans of bad sexual news every three or four months, tell us a lot about our hidden selves, certainly. But if we look less closely, removing our gaze from our navels and glancing at the pile of magazines and the endless "news" stories, which enrich such pitiful lads, we can begin to see the targets for our ire. Who are the villains of the piece? Is this twisted view of boys and men acceptable?

So what am I going to do about it?

Looking deeper, we see boys who are just one step over a line that the boys we know can clearly see. In the community, who are the heroes? Who are the wimps? Who are the victims? Who is excluded? Are the boys in the community learning compassion or are they learning cruelty? Do the men see the pain of the boys?

SO WHAT ARE WE GOING TO DO ABOUT IT?

A mindful day.

This is a day of mindfulness. What is sought here is not a unique day, standing distinctly apart from all others, but a day when the practice of mindfulness moves into the foreground. Today is a day of enrichment and heightened awareness. Please bring this wonderful practice into every day.

Mindfulness is not an esoteric practice. Being mindful simply means being awake. For men, being mindful can mean the beginning of the end of the social masculine trance and the dismembered life. In mindfulness we become aware of the fullness and flow of our lives, one moment at a time.

The Appendix of this book contains specific directions and suggestions. I encourage you to visit a library or bookstore for additional help in this ancient practice. One excellent book is *Full Catastrophe Living* by Jon Kabat-Zinn, Ph.D. The Vietnamese Buddhist monk Thich Naht Hahn has written dozens of books, many of which concern mindfulness. My personal favorites are *The Miracle of Mindfulness* and *Being Peace*.

This is a beautiful day. Please embrace it fully.

July 8

There's sort of that frailty in mankind that's very interesting to explore. Heroics are so few and far between.
—CLINT EASTWOOD

In recent years, we men have begun to think of ourselves in different ways—some new, driven by the times, and some ancient, driven by myth and prayer. We have broken free of the tyranny of man as the worker bee, driven and aloof. We see our homes not as our castles, but as our centers, sites of communion and love. We are driven as much by our hearts as by our minds.

We must be vigilant. We do not acquire wholeness. Wholeness is revealed. The full life of a man is not an accomplishment, it is a gift.

Begun heroically, the journey does not end in heroics and, in time, it becomes the task of humility and gratitude to lead us home.

In time, the king becomes the servant. The warrior becomes the guardian. The magician becomes the storyteller, and the lover, the gardener.

🌳 🌳 🌳

I WILL STRIVE TO PUT AN END TO MERE HEROICS.

July 9

For the whole law is contained in one word, "You shall love your neighbor as yourself."
—GALATIANS 5:14

We are not alone. In the process of awakening and of conscious masculine living, we must discover who our neighbors are. Who lives in our neighborhoods? To whom do we extend our hearts and our hands? What do we require of another in order to include her? Are we willing to be patient? Forgiving? Is it okay to feel anger at a neighbor as we get to know him? Who were we "taught to hate and fear"? What was "drummed in our dear little ear"? Are these people our neighbors?

Who does not belong?

The re-membered man expands his kinship, creating real communities that seek diversity rather than monotony. He sees his neighbor, as well, in distant lands, with unfamiliar customs and traditions. He grows in love in large degree as he grows in neighbors.

WHO IS MY NEIGHBOR? WHO IS NOT?

July 10

Everybody in the world has the sensation of being tied down hand and foot—everyone has his own private bloodsucker.
—UGO BETTI

In our private moments, often, it is said, at three o'clock in the morning, the most confident of us can be scraped raw, on the inside, by feelings of inadequacy, incompetence, or simple, choking dread. As Scrooge would have it, perhaps it sometimes is only "a bit of undigested beef" (or too much chocolate ice cream) but more often there is some genuine haunting discontent or lingering fear that bedevils us.

For years, men have felt guilty about such quiverings of the heart. We "shouldn't" feel like this. And yet we did feel like that and part of our dis-ease was a stubborn refusal to talk openly and honestly about our "weakness."

As we are becoming energized once more, open, imaginative, and spirited, we see the value in sharing these feelings with others. Shame evaporates. We accept that in fact we are inadequate to some tasks. We see that dread lives only in the unknown future.

WE ARE HEALED AS THE HEALER IS HEALED.

July 11

We have eaten ourselves all the way up to our necks.
—CHRIS GOEDECKE

Our hunger has been so great that we finally began devouring ourselves. At the expense of our bodies and spirits, we accumulated information and its rapacious brother, power. We denied the wisdom of the senses and the desires of the heart. The results were woeful.

As we are being transformed, we are putting ourselves together in new ways. Our centers are not in our minds, or localized in the penis or the throat. The men who began to colonize time have fled those frontiers and are recolonizing their own bodies. The energy is flowing again and our bodies are joyful. When we move, we feel the breeze we make. When we are struck, we feel the pain, but do not imagine an insult. When we make love, our spirits rise to orgasm. When we see pain in others, we feel it in ourselves.

The awakened body carries us, sensuously and powerfully, along paths the mind can never find.

TODAY IS A DAY OF SKINFUL PLEASURE.

July 12

To keep oneself safe, does not mean to bury oneself.
—SENECA

We grew up in a world that we were told was unsafe. My peers grew up learning to "duck and cover"; places of learning or of worship became bomb shelters once a week. Our fathers worked hard to make our homes secure, but forgot how to comfort us with words and touch. Younger men now have seen great leaders murdered and have said good-bye a final time to friends and lovers wasted by a new and awful plague.

We long to be safe. Men are now called not to run to safety but to provide it. As the warrior role is replaced by the guardian role, we are becoming safe by taking risks. In hiding we empowered the predator; by living fully, we are empowering our neighbors.

❦ ❦ ❦

THE COWARDLY MAN BUILDS A TOMB AND CALLS IT HOME.

If I do not acknowledge my teachers, their teachings can fade. I will practice mindful recollection of them all.

LIST YOUR TEACHERS.

July 14

He who would learn to fly one day must first learn to stand and walk and run and climb and dance; one cannot fly into flying.
—FRIEDRICH NIETZSCHE

We have all seen, or perhaps been, men who understand so quickly that they never are able to learn. Just so, anyone with a pocket calculator can do complicated mathematics. Not so long ago, we sought enlightenment by swallowing tiny multicolored tablets. We said we wanted to destroy our egos at a time before we had had time to develop an ego to destroy.

Awakening to our pasts as boys and men is a time-consuming chore; the work of the rest of a lifetime. We must be careful not to stumble over the old obstacles that broke our stride and, finally, our spirits, years ago. So we need to lose sight of our goals rather than race toward them heedlessly, never glancing away from them. We need to take time; more time than the time we think we need to take.

MEN'S TASKS ARE CRUCIAL, AND THEY ARE URGENT. WE SERVE THEM BEST BY MOVING SLOWLY AND GENTLY.

July 15

What is important is truth and being a just man. If I can live in truth, then I will be taken care of.
—TOM BROWN, JR.

When a man is lost in the storm of his desires and fears, truth can often seem a luxury or, at best, something to be negotiated in the process of accumulation or flight. We do not behave justly when we are fearful or dishonest. Justice requires the cessation of ego-driven needs. Yet living this life of fear and desire ended in depression and what Bill Wilson called "anxious apartness," with the god-shaped hole still empty.

Then we began to discover that other men were lost and afraid, living with great doubts about their direction, beliefs, and purpose. As we began to talk truthfully with each other, from the heart, we found love and understanding where there had always been fear and competition. Becoming vulnerable with other men has been healing rather than threatening. We crave justice and so we practice it, just as we speak our truth to hear it from our brothers.

SLY MANIPULATION IS NO VIRTUE. WE WERE PERISHING INSIDE OUR SELFISH ARMOR.

July 16

All men should strive to learn before they die what they are running from, and to, and why.
—James Thurber

Watch the people on the streets today. Stop yourself and see how they run. It is unlikely that all of us, rushing about as we do, are really motivated simply by getting to that meeting or that lunch or that assignation or the bus home. There is clearly some deeper urgency these days that propels us to such a scattered and worried pace.

A priest once told me that if he ever got to heaven it would be as a result of running away from hell. Nobler than most. And clearer. Could it be that that hell is the one we create in our own minds, fueled with fear and peopled by parents, family, and other critics, all of our own making? Perhaps.

Many men didn't know they were running until a friend, who had slowed down, said, "Don't rush so. Let's sit down. Let me tell you a story." And these men were startled to hear that there are ways of being in the world that are easier paced and more gentle to the soul. They found, at a slower pace, that no one was chasing them. They learned that it is possible to live purposefully without running.

I'LL LOOK BACK TODAY AND NOTICE THAT
NOTHING IS GAINING ON ME.

July 17

The body repeats the landscape. They are the source of each other and create each other.
—MERIDEL LE SUEUR

Both science and religion are now claiming to see proof of the deep interconnectedness of all things.

Common sense will do the same. As I eat the vegetables from my garden and drink the water from the Esopus reservoir, that garden and those mountains around the reservoir become part of me. My waste becomes part of my garden and of those mountains.

I can no longer endure the delusion of being separate. That conceit evaporates when I hold my wife's hand or walk in the garden with my son. The day I became a formal student of Zen Buddhism, the trees around my home shimmered in celebration.

TODAY I WILL CONSIDER THE BOUNDARIES AROUND
THIS SEPARATE SELF.

July 18

For all the pseudo-sophistication of twentieth century sex theory, it is still assumed that a man should make love as if his principal intention was to people the wilderness.
—GERMAINE GREER

We screwed like beasts for years; avid in the pursuit, anxious in the act, depressed the moment after. In spite of what we said, we were not making love, we were making war. We were play*boys*, not playful men. We demeaned our partners and ourselves.

Men are learning that sex does not need to be about power. We are seeing that, in the words of Robert Aitken, "the home is healed in the marriage bed." We are also seeing that surrendering to true eroticism and sensualism re-sensitizes the body to exquisite and undreamed-of pleasures.

WHEN SEXUAL FEELINGS ARISE TODAY, I WILL LOOK DEEPLY AT THEM. ARE THEY ABOUT POWER, ABOUT ADDICTION, ABOUT ESCAPE? I CAN SEE THAT THEY REVEAL MY HUMANITY, NOT A SICKNESS.

July 19

To be good is noble, but to teach others how to be good is nobler—and less trouble.
—MARK TWAIN

My daughter once reminded me to be careful not to get hungry, angry, lonely, or tired. I, her father and teacher after all, archly reminded her that the cliché, which I had taught her, says not to get "too" hungry, etc. She replied tenderly that she was well aware of how it was worded but that in my case the way she said it was the way she meant it. And she was right. It took me awhile to forgive her for that.

As we look more deeply at our behaviors, we can't help but be more careful about our teachings. It is not hypocrisy that is the concern here, but the loss of our own moral bearings. When we are honest with ourselves, we are forced into compassion for others. When we are willing to look silly in our own eyes, we become so much more human in the eyes of others.

WHEN I BEGIN TO SCRUTINIZE OTHERS TODAY, I WILL CONSIDER HOW WELL I WOULD BEAR UP UNDER THAT STARE.

July 20

Listen, or thy tongues will keep thee deaf.
—NATIVE AMERICAN PROVERB

A ten-year-old boy was assaulted by a substitute teacher in a classroom in a school in a fashionable section of rural New Jersey. The director of the school assured the boy's parents that he would go and talk to the class about what had happened. The parents, with one voice, said, "No! You go and *listen* to them about it." Their hearts knew what all the director's studies had never told him; that we serve best by our listening, not by our telling.

Those of us who had fathers who didn't listen learned that not listening was the way of a man. If we did see ourselves mirrored in our father's open and loving face, rapt with attention at the talk of a young boy, we never knew who we were. If our talk was cut off or dismissed, parts of us were amputated. We grew up as talkers, fixers, analyzers, and pedants. We were so quick to explain that the depths were never revealed. There is too much ambiguity and uncertainty in simply listening. It made us uncomfortable. "I hear you," we said, jumping in in midsentence.

Today we can trust ourselves as listeners. The men's movement has begun to break the pedagogy of the patriarch. We listen to each other and reach beyond the circle to hear what is straining to be said by those who need our strength.

I CAN LISTEN WITH MY HEART WITHOUT BREAKING IT.

A mindful day.

This is a day of mindfulness. What is sought here is not a unique day, standing distinctly apart from all others, but a day when the practice of mindfulness moves into the foreground. Today is a day of enrichment and heightened awareness. Please bring this wonderful practice into every day.

Mindfulness is not an esoteric practice. Being mindful simply means being awake. For men, being mindful can mean the beginning of the end of the social masculine trance and the dismembered life. In mindfulness we become aware of the fullness and flow of our lives, one moment at a time.

The Appendix of this book contains specific directions and suggestions. I encourage you to visit a library or bookstore for additional help in this ancient practice. One excellent book is *Full Catastrophe Living* by Jon Kabat-Zinn, Ph.D. The Vietnamese Buddhist monk Thich Naht Hahn has written dozens of books, many of which concern mindfulness. My personal favorites are *The Miracle of Mindfulness* and *Being Peace*.

This is a beautiful day. Please embrace it fully.

July 22

There are people in my life who have added to who I am by their presence and love. Recalling them honors them and adds to my strength. They are in my story.

WRITE A LETTER TO YOUR BROTHER OR SISTER, BLOOD OR SOUL.

July 23

If you are what you do, and then you don't, you aren't.
—Robert Subby

Perhaps men should start carrying *pleasure* cards rather than *business* cards. The line under the name could read father, gardener, eroticist, poet, storyteller, sailor, or dreamer. Make your own list. We could also call these our *gut* or our *bliss* cards. For the awakening man, they are all student cards in any case.

Certainly, men's identities have been too tied up in only a few dimensions of their lives and all too often, these are solely active dimensions. We were not only our jobs, we were also our "leisure" activities. Imagine a card that says Architect and Shopper.

These are lightweight ruminations about a deadly subject. Look at the men in your life who have died or suffered serious health problems shortly after "retiring." My father had a massive heart attack only two months after ending a forty-year career as an educator and writer. Some men descend into alcoholism or other of the visible addictions when they lose their jobs. Often, they are blamed for their short-sightedness. It is our job to grieve for them and help them. They were no different from any of us who have built our identities around our social role.

It is our job, in addition, to put an end to the charade of the human doing and to celebrate the human being.

July 24

You show me a man who has no men he admires, I'll show you a man whose Trickster is running over all the time.
—ROBERT MOORE

The trickster here is the healthy skeptic. He's the distancing one, the coyote with a porno habit or the infant Krishna never grown up. Fully functional, he keeps us away from the cults and the gurus; he bursts the idealism before it becomes fatally inflated. Good for the trickster.

Men often are overly distant and skeptical. Judging cynically and keeping one's distance are adaptive strategies that have served many of us well in a world seen as hostile and godless. But when the trickster motor is on auto, we are turned off to one of our greatest resources—other men, wiser, older perhaps, more loving—who can be our teachers and models.

Consider the men you admire. Some of mine are Sam Keen, Dean James Morton (at Saint John the Divine), Lenny Holzer, and Senator Bill Bradley. My original list, when I first began this work included, for example, Zorro and Albert Einstein, a comic book figure, and a dead man. As I go on, I suspect that these men will be closer to me yet—distance will evaporate until I can count as those I admire Ron, Ken, Mark, and Herb, founding members of the Convent Men's Group.

MEN I ADMIRE, CLOSE UP, ENRICH ME AND MIRROR ME.

He who has to walk with fools has a long journey of sorrow ...
but the joy of being with the wise is like the joy of meeting a be-
loved kinsman.
—THE DHAMMAPADA

Today we do not need to be in the company of fools. We can lovingly detach from the manipulators, the warlike, the addicted, and the chronic critics. These are not our enemies; we are leaving the illness, not the person. If our brothers are in pain, we can help them as we heal by our example of healing.

The path of growth and change is illuminated by those who have gone ahead of us, if only a little distance. Their wisdom is in their experience. It is our task to ask them to share it. This does not come easy to many men. We are hesitant to ask because we might look weak or incompetent. They might say no. They might be the wrong person. What if they tell? These barriers do not occur before the journey; they are part of it. To walk in the company of the wise, we must be willing to be not-wise. To learn from the masters, we must be willing to be beginners.

Our old disspirited selves could not imagine the joy and the power of walking with the elders. The tradition was lost but not murdered. The spirited man has remembered it and, doing so, has entered a process of transformation and renewal.

I CAN LEARN TO LISTEN TO THE ELDERS
BY NOT LISTENING TO THE FOOLS.

July 26

They order things so damnably in hell.
—HILAIRE BELLOC

I am an orderly person. Until I began this men's work and began to recover my spontaneity and imagination and could let go of obsessive control, what my wife saw as comfortable funkiness, I saw as sloth and chaos. (Now I only see an irritating mess.)

It's so heavily patriarchal, this overscheduling, shelf-tidying, list-making, catalogue-thumbing obsession with obscuring every moment and event of the day. We had the Power, because our Daytimers were loaded, our Powerbooks were on line all the time, and the ketchup was kept where the ketchup belonged. On the weekends, we knew we were not to work but to play—so we planned our playing. During the week, we knew were not to play but to work. "All work and no play makes Jack . . ." So work we did, every *i* dotted, every *t* crossed, every moment missed.

In learning to let go, we are undermining the patri-arch, internal and external. We are more comfortable with uncertainty and ambiguity. Our lives are expansive and delightful, filled with unanticipated joy and spontaneous gasps of awe at the wonder of unscheduled and unlisted events.

🌿 🌿 🌿

HAVE I SCHEDULED JOY TODAY?

His father watched him across the gulf of years and pathos which always must divide a father from his son.
—J.P. MARQUAND

As fathers, we must not see our children as reflections of ourselves, or as clay to be molded to a certain shape. We cannot understand their experience, finally, nor expect them to understand ours. We can give them our experience, however, to refract through their own. Starting at an early age, earlier than we think reasonable, we can begin to tell them stories. No matter how made-up or fantastic these stories may seem to us, they nonetheless contain ancient wisdom and great chunks of our own souls. As we tell our stories to our children, they are incorporating them. My tales of my pony named Dolly are part of Willie's experience now.

As sons, we can ask our fathers to tell us stories as well. Because my father has told me some of his tales, I know more about western Tennessee than I ever could have found in a book.

There are many stories for our children to hear. Television, movies, and storybooks are full of them. Now we are questioning who the real storyteller should be in our homes.

WHO ARE THE STORYTELLERS IN MY COMMUNITY?
WHERE AM I ON THAT LIST?

July 28

If you haven't lived the life, it won't come out the horn.
—CHARLES MINGUS

Disconnected from our bodies and our stories, we were liable to say almost anything. It is a gift to be able to think rationally, coldly, and clearly. That ability has led us to great breakthroughs and is not to be disparaged. Exercised alone, however, divorced from realization (i.e., from being made real), it has also led to break*downs.*

Men are forming communities where they tell each other their stories, sharing experience rather than ideas. We are finding a common taproot that goes deeper than any thought has ever led us, into the soil of the soul. There we are realizing our lives and uncovering both our suffering, from years of isolation, and our compassion, born of that suffering.

Many of us have had the experience of helping friends or family in new and surprising ways. A man whose daughter is in serious trouble with drugs and alcohol tells her the story of his life of addiction. He tells his story openly, without moralizing or advising, trusting her beyond doubt, and feels the healing of ancient wounds as their hearts open to each other.

❦ ❦ ❦

I'VE LIVED "THE LIFE." HAVE I NOTICED IT?

July 29

We abuse land because we regard it as a commodity belonging to us. When we see land as a community to which we belong, we may begin to use it with love and respect.
—ALDO LEOPOLD

Our isolation from the land has led to a wounding that many feel may never heal. We have poisoned our children's gardens for greener lawns. We have uprooted oxygen-giving trees for backyard swimming pools. We have dirtied our neighbors' lungs by driving, alone, on highways paralleling railroads that lead to the same destinations. Eager for diversion, we have tried to convert great parcels of wild lands into woodsy Disneylands, managed and safe.

The early women's movement taught us that "the personal is political." Now we need to see that the personal is the ecological. In poisoning the land, we are literally poisoning ourselves. In respecting the natural community, we are respecting ourselves.

We need to see where we can make changes that make changes, close at hand or in our towns, schools, and larger communities. For example, what is being taught in the local Boy Scouts? Could a men's group provide an alternative?

TODAY, AT THE MOMENT WHEN I AM TOO BUSY, I WILL TAKE A MOMENT AND CONSIDER WHAT MY BUDDIES AND I CAN DO FOR THE EARTH UNDER OUR FEET.

July 30

We are monumentally distracted by a pervasive technological culture that appears to have a life of its own, one that insists on our full attention, continually seducing us and pulling us away from the opportunity to experience directly the true meaning of our own lives.
—AL GORE

At home, there are clocks on appliances, never in synch; there are miles of wire connecting "entertainment" devices. Outside, carbon arc lamps chase away the dark, more miles of wire bring the world humming and screaming into our homes. We have devices that create power for more devices to consume. An endless line of kilowatts and megabytes chews up our attention.

It wasn't so long ago that every month or so would bring news of a "crazed" man who got down his shotgun and blew his TV set away. One can imagine the neighbors' reaction. "He was such a quiet man. Never caused any trouble at all. Stayed to himself. Loved his TV and his family. I'm shocked. How could he have done such a thing?"

How can we resist doing such a thing?

Hide the car keys, disconnect every clock in the house, unplug the entertainment toys, turn off the lights, neutralize the phone (and not with an answering machine), dismantle the alarm and electric fence, and spend just one day talking with your partners. Tell your story. Make up songs. Write poems. Be scared. Sit quietly.

HOW CAN WE RESIST DOING SUCH A THING?

When I find I am merely thinking about my story I will resolutely turn to the memories of my senses and know my life with my entire being.

WRITE ABOUT THE MOST POTENT SCENT OF YOUR CHILDHOOD.

August 1

The first of this month is Lammas, the day halfway between the summer solstice and the autumnal equinox. This is the time of the earth's final preparation for the seeds that will fall at harvest for winter germination.

This is a month of preparation for change and of hope for future abundance. The Hopi Snake Dance Festival is held in August, a time of prayer for rain to nourish the earth.

In Hinduism, the birth of Krishna is celebrated (Janmashtame).

August 2

He (a man) becomes a reservoir of aggression on which society can draw to produce its goods competitively, fight its wars fiercely, and raise children more aggressive than himself.
—HOLMES WELCH

An advertising executive in Manhattan, at a strategy session dealing with how to overcome a client's anger, says, "We could just tell them we're sorry."

An athletic third-grader, under pressure to play soccer five afternoons a week, plus weekend games, as his school requires, says no and wonders why they don't have science classes five days a week as well.

His brother drops out of the Boy Scouts because he wants to be gentle in the forests and is offended by the games the scouts play, which are violent and unrelated to the natural environment. He also says he doesn't like having to pledge allegiance to a flag and to talk of a Christian God he does not believe in.

A banking executive, at forty, drops out to become an archivist for a nonprofit organization.

WHAT IF SOME MEN SAID,
"WE WON'T FIGHT YOUR WARS ANYMORE"?

August 3

Neither the country nor the society we built out of it can be healthy until we stop raiding and running, and learn to be quiet part of the time, and acquire the sense not of ownership but of belonging.
—WALLACE STEGNER

When we take time to see where we are, we begin to see what we are. It is difficult to spend a few hours simply trying to catch the rhythms of the day and not become right-sized. A day's walk in the park with a child, or a few days in the nearby wilderness without gadgets, begins to restore the balance and right proportion that years of "raiding and running" destroyed.

Men are reconsidering what "patriotism" is about. Are we loyal to a flag? Do we fight our wars by tying ribbons to trees or flying flags on our cars or stickering their bumpers?

We are seeing there is a deeper loyalty to this country and society that starts with the land itself and our total interpenetration with it, and that considers the hearts of children, patriots all, raised on televised wars. By looking hard at our own lives, admitting our own mistakes, and setting a moral course, we are telling our children to honor the earth and serve it, and to see that those who die to our cheers subtract from our lives as well.

THERE IS NO LONGER ENOUGH TIME TO BE IN A HURRY.

August 4

Forgive us . . . for pasting stained glass on our eyes and our ears to shut out the cry of the hungry and the hurt of the world.
—UNITED PRESBYTERIAN CHURCH
Litany for Holy Communion, 1968

Without the experience of our own suffering, we could not feel the suffering of others. We men, shut off from the neck down, were skilled at doing the "mind work" of the community or the church and remained untrained to weep at the daily images of pain we saw in the newspapers, magazines, and television programs. We were hurt nonetheless, and in returning to community and to wholeness, the pain we had unknowingly endured surfaced.

We ask forgiveness by our actions now. As the folk saying goes, we "get up off our knees and put legs on our prayers." Rather than telling others what to do, we tell them what we have done in circumstances like theirs. Rather than being outraged at injustice, we pick our battles and set out to make a real difference in a real world, thick with pain and love.

The men's movement is not political. Many men involved in this leaderless arising are becoming politicized. We see we cannot heal ourselves without healing our world.

WE'RE BREAKING OUT THE STAINED GLASS WINDOWS AND INVITING THE WORLD INSIDE.

August 5

We can choose to live our lives buttoned up and secure, dead from the necktie down, comfortable, well furnished, and sniffy. Our solitude wears well and often invisibly in our home, our workplace, and our community.

ISOLATED, I'M IN QUESTIONABLE COMPANY.

August 6

It is a strange desire to seek power and to lose liberty.
—FRANCIS BACON

One configuration of a contemporary jail looks like this: a large, well-decorated central building, with satellite dish, custom electronic amusement center, a three-acre exercise yard with swimming pool, and a recreation room—the whole of it surrounded by an electric fence and protected by sensitive alarms. The inmates are a successful man and his family.

In accumulating both material power and the more evanescent and heady power of inclusion in a small and powerful group, we had to learn anger and prejudice. And along the way we sacrificed compassion. The patriarchal culture provided the illusion of power and locked the gates of bejeweled prisons. We were the prisoners of greed, dispirited and isolated.

We have "put pennies in our shoes" now. We are returning to earth, both in spirit and in fact. The enchantment of money, sex, and power is being broken as men talk with men about their secret sadnesses, long unacknowledged.

THE ILLUSION OF POWER IS BEING REPLACED BY THE POWER OF FREEDOM OF BODY, MIND, AND SPIRIT.

August 7

A mindful day.

This is a day of mindfulness. What is sought here is not a unique day, standing distinctly apart from all others, but a day when the practice of mindfulness moves into the foreground. Today is a day of enrichment and heightened awareness. Please bring this wonderful practice into every day.

Mindfulness is not an esoteric practice. Being mindful simply means being awake. For men, being mindful can mean the beginning of the end of the social masculine trance and the dismembered life. In mindfulness we become aware of the fullness and flow of our lives, one moment at a time.

The Appendix of this book contains specific directions and suggestions. I encourage you to visit a library or bookstore for additional help in this ancient practice. One excellent book is *Full Catastrophe Living* by Jon Kabat-Zinn, Ph.D. The Vietnamese Buddhist monk Thich Naht Hahn has written dozens of books, many of which concern mindfulness. My personal favorites are *The Miracle of Mindfulness* and *Being Peace.*

This is a beautiful day. Please embrace it fully.

August 8

The paradox of courage is that a man must be a little careless of his life even in order to keep it.
—G. K. Chesterton

A man need not be faithful, at forty, to a rigid life course he set upon at twenty. Here are the questions we are asking now: Why should we be held hostage to the romanticism and cynicism of youth? Where is the flexibility that is demanded by the unexpected blessing? Can we trust our partners to support us rather than fearing they will leave us if we become "a little careless" of our lives? Can our intuition be followed, no matter what the risk?

Our culture demands that we produce and to that end it provides carrot ("do right and you get the gold watch . . . early") and stick ("do wrong and you will be deemed inadequate, unmanly, dickless").

Can we continue to honor that contract?

🌿 🌿 🌿

CAN WE TURN OUR BACKS ON THE PATRIARCHAL CULTURE AND
NURTURE OUR FAMILIES AND COMMUNITIES? CAN WE PRACTICE
FAITH RATHER THAN FEAR?

August 9

If men do not keep on speaking terms with children,
they cease to be men, and become merely machines
for eating and for earning money.
—JOHN UPDIKE

Many men made life choices early on that they follow to this day, happily and productively. There is no secret sorrow. Such a man is, as Joseph Campbell counseled, following his bliss. Most often, these are the men who received a blessing from a parent or mentor. They were offered the gift of perspective, rather than the burden of obligation. Their education was a matter of learning to think and to feel, to know good from evil, rather than learning to produce. In their families, often, it was the adults who performed for the children, rather than children for the adults.

We teach by who we are, not by what we say. When we examine our own lives, we see what our fathers taught us. Do we want to pass that on?

Do we want to be men? Can we put an end now to the teaching of aggression and conformity and begin to teach freedom? Being on speaking terms with children, are we willing to listen as well, and to learn?

WHAT ARE MY TEACHINGS?

August 10

What grows in solitude then goes back into the community.
—RUTH COOKE

In solitude, there is a sense of something missing so we move back to community. In community there is a piece gone, so we move back to solitude. In the balance, our lives are played out with serenity and power.

Solitude is other than isolation. Isolation depends on addiction for its strength; it is a shutting down, while solitude is an opening up. Men have known isolation too well and solitude not at all. The *Tao te Ching* says that we can open to the world without opening our front door. That is, the world is within us and can be experienced in solitude. This is a religious practice, a practice of connecting to the source, but it is incomplete without a return to community. Solitude is fruitful and we are obliged to carry the fruits of solitude to the community.

Community is other than proximity. Proximity is often accidental and although it may be part of community it still depends on walls for its strength; it exludes, while community includes. Community is enriched by the solitude of its members, while proximity can be improverished by their isolation.

WE SEEK COMMUNITY AND SOLITUDE.

August 11

When I find I can recite the television schedule or name the vineyards of the most chic pressings, I will humbly turn to the larger world about me and get right-sized. What have I forgotten?

FIND OUT THE NAME OF ONE TREE, BUSH, OR SHRUB YOU SEE EVERY DAY.

Life without a friend; death without a witness.
—GEORGE HERBERT

Some have suggested that what men really want is friends. We had friends when we were boys, most of us; we had boy friends whom we rode our bikes with at dusk, in the cool breezes or whom we went backyard camping with. During some of our boyhood times, we had erotic play with other boys, touching each other, watching and comparing, being close and secretive. There was usually some boy friend we talked with about God and girls. If we lacked such friends, we were injured.

Time passed. We were busy getting on, moving up; priorities changed. We had ambition and responsibility. Society didn't value "male bonding." In some cases, a homophobic society frightened us away from other men, gay or straight. We saw our friends fade to the background.

Yet now, if we lack male friends, we simply shrug and say that things change and, yeah, I've got some friends but I've got a family now, you know. We don't acknowledge the hurt and the longing, but we look long at the men we know who have close friends and the boy in us feels an empty place, friend-shaped.

THERE IS A WAY BACK TO MALE FRIENDSHIP. THE JOURNEY IS EASY ONCE BEGUN. SUCCESS IS INEVITABLE.

August 13

Wishing to be friends is quick work, but friendship is a slow-ripening fruit.
—ARISTOTLE

My doctor, a wise and literate man, had as another client a very famous man, a novelist, who died too young and too lonely. Dr. McCormack said that the man "... lacked an essential skill. He could not go through the process of becoming a friend. You were either his friend or not, on first meeting." In hearing the truth about this man, I was hearing the truth about myself. I had no friends with whom I had developed a friendship. There were many instant friendships, based always on some one commonality, one place where our minds or habits touched. Drinking buddies, for example, or editors. Democrats, dropouts, and drug dealers. Instant friends, disposable and replaceable.

In the years since that epiphany, I told the story to many men and the great majority of them have had a reaction much like mine. Along the way, we lost the skill of *becoming* a friend. We were too wary, too ambitious, too lost in acquiring and consuming.

We are rediscovering those skills now, like boys back on a bicycle the day after an ugly fall. Becoming a friend is not something we learn; it is something we recover. The rhythms, the watching, the pleasure and the pain are as familiar as the scent of whiskey or honeysuckle.

WE ARE GIVING OUR FRIENDS THE GIFTS OF
PATIENCE AND FORGIVENESS.

I loathe a friend whose gratitude grows old
a friend who takes his friend's prosperity
but will not voyage with him in his grief.
—EURIPIDES

"Nobody loves you when you're down and out" is the maudlin refrain of a blues song. As important as it is to be with a friend who is grieving, it is more important still to let him grieve completely. We cannot stand to see others suffer; we want to relieve their pain quickly because it reminds us so vividly of our own. When our friend is in his personal darkness, we dishonor him and our friendship by trying to lead him out prematurely. His wounds will not heal—he will be left with unspoken sorrow and the low ache of unminded sores.

When our friend is in grief, we go *with* him; we do not lead or push. His comfort is in our presence, silent and close. When the time comes we can share stories about our bad times and tell him about what was born there.

BEING A FRIEND IS ABOUT LETTING GO.

August 15

It is the province of knowledge to speak and it is the privilege of wisdom to listen.
—OLIVER WENDELL HOLMES

A man whose wife and five children were killed in a shoot-out ending in an inferno said that the authorities did the best they could and that that was the worst. He went on to say that all parties concerned used everything they had, except wisdom.

Wisdom is earned rather than learned, but when we pay attention to the quiet promptings of intuition and conscience, the well of wisdom is uncovered. It is deep even in the least experienced of us. We access wisdom in the silent mind, not the noisy one. Our wisdom is revealed when we are attentively passive, faith-filled and without ego-driven ideas.

How many men have rushed into situations when help was called for using only their knowledge, leaving wisdom behind in the swirl of ego-dust kicked up by fear and uncertainty?

What have the results been?

With the ego out of the way and self-centered fear not leading our actions, we are useful in ways we had not known possible. We can exercise patience, humility, and acceptance in situations that previously were met with panic and power.

WHAT ARE THE RESULTS?

August 16

Happiness and Beauty are by-products.
—GEORGE BERNARD SHAW

Happiness has been a learned goal, the payoff for most of us. We say "When I get __, then I'll be happy" or "If only __, I'd be happy." We accumulated toys; cars; record players; five different kinds of telephones, stationary and mobile; wives and girlfriends—all *in order* to be happy.

The accumulation of material things is, of course, not the only path men have taken to the happiness crossbars. Some of us embraced the spiritual life *in order* to be happy. "If I just meet my quota of good works, then . . ." or "Buddhists laugh a lot so if I'm a Buddhist, then . . ." and on and on.

Has it worked?

Why were we so unhappy to begin with? Who taught us this unhappiness that we dreaded so? Where had this happiness gone that it became a goal rather than a way of being, coincidental with a healthy, loving, sharing life?

TODAY I WILL MAKE ONE PERSON HAPPY.

August 17

If you imagine that once you have accomplished your ambitions you will have time to turn to the Way, you will discover that your ambitions never come to an end.

—YOSHIDA KENKO

When we were serving our ambitions, we lost our anchors; the more ambitious we became, the further we drifted from center, the more fragmented and dissipirited we became until, finally, narcotized by goods and achievement, though living we stood at the threshold of death. Yet our lives had not become intolerable and we were not in pain—any longer. We were, rather, complacent. Drugged. Hypnotized. Our ambitions were reborn daily, in new and delicious forms.

Something happened then. The spirit would not die, cannot die, some say. That part of us which refuses to perish began to thrust upward, to the light, as it has in the past in times of war or other great physical danger. Our courage and our power were reborn in the face of this reaper of the twentieth century, who whispered gently of comfort rather than roaring with cannons and rage. We could no longer turn our faces from the suffering we saw and, confronting it, our own suffering became known. Our Way reappeared, instantly and with great clarity. It had lain, for most of our lives, just beneath the thin disguise of ambition and need.

HOW MANY OF US WANT THE SPIRITUAL LIFE?
HOW MANY OF US NEED IT?

August 18

So the darkness shall be the light, and the stillness the dancing.
—T.S. ELIOT

One of the great challenges of the new men's work is to put aside our old impatience in waiting for a predetermined result. We can't always know where we are headed. If we could see the future, we wouldn't have gotten ourselves caught in these boxes in the first place.

We cannot stand uncertainty or disorder. A messy house often seems to threaten chaos, and an "undisciplined" child carries with her the threat of insanity. We have lived wanting to be in control. Control, we see from simple experience, is an illusion.

Now we need patience and acceptance only. As Eliot says elsewhere in this poem ("East Coker"), we must wait without hope, love, faith, or thought. All but thought would be for the wrong thing, and we "are not yet ready for thought."

TO DANCE, SIT STILL. TO SEE, COVER YOUR EYES.

August 19

Ordinary objects are not very ordinary when seen mindfully. When I am bored by the ordinariness of my world, I will look more deeply and read the stories there.

August 20

Until he extends his circle of compassion to all living things, man will not himself find peace.
—ALBERT SCHWEITZER

What circles do we draw around ourselves? Who is excluded from our caring? What is excluded from our caring?

When we give parties, who is on the guest list? If we made a list of people we didn't invite, and wrote out the reasons in every case, would we feel peace or dis-ease?

Whom do we punish by not sending them holiday cards?

Who is allowed to die or to live in suffering so that we can feel comfortable?

Which children are not in our circle of compassion?

CAN WE FIND PEACE WHILE THEY ARE WATCHING?

August 21

I hope the leaders of the YMCA start a campaign to induce good young men to do nothing.
—BERTRAND RUSSELL

Some men were encouraged or, better, empowered, to do nothing. And doing nothing, they became skilled at it. The majority of men, however, have never developed the ability to do nothing.

Doing nothing usually doesn't last very long. Send a boy into the park to sit on a bench and do nothing, and within moments a blade of grass will tremble as an ant brushes it, walking by carrying a load of corn chip home. That ant. Where could its home be? What does it look like? What if I took that piece of food away? Was it the ant or the wind that moved the grass? Look at the way the ant's legs move.

Imagination is born here. Boredom dies, and reverence begins.

IN A CULTURE CONSUMED WITH GETTING AND MOVING,
ONE EYE ON THE CLOCK AND THE OTHER ON THE ENEMY,
CAN WE EMPOWER OUR YOUNG PEOPLE TO LEARN
THE EXQUISITE SKILL OF DOING NOTHING?

August 22

*All miseries derive from not being able to sit quietly
in a room alone.*
—PASCAL

We have developed some very sophisticated neuro-muscular responses to sudden solitude. We walk into an empty room and within moments have turned on the television. We find ourselves, without having thought of it, standing mesmerized, channel-surfing, pausing only for seconds on each electronic offering until we find a comforting one, usually "the news." Failing that, we turn on the radio, make a phone call, or just call out for someone nearby.

Is there something in silence that threatens us? What or who is it that we are afraid might be in there with us?

Men who have a regular practice of meditation, just quietly sitting alone, talk of the great power of this silent time. They begin to seek the quiet rather than avoid it, and see solitude as a gift. It is not that they learn to *use* the time but that they learn to value it. This is a time to step away from the riot of the discursive mind, to observe thought, to feel the beginnings of serenity, to reclaim one's life from the cacophony of other people's busywork.

INSIGHT IS THE GIFT OF A QUIET MIND.

August 23

My books are the brooks, my sermons the stones
my parson's a wolf on a pulpit of bones.
—ALAN MCCANLESS
(cowboy poet, late 1800s)

We know we've lost the sense of the rhythms of the planet, the long play of light and dark, the sounds of the hunter and prey in their habitat—and ours—just out of sight. We have grown impoverished and saddened and have turned in endless circles to find the road back to these basic riches.

There is a cathedral nearby. A library looms beside it, choking with books, and in back of it is a vast savanna, violently alive and humming.

Our *places*, where we are, are our cathedrals, libraries, savannas, and retreats. We had lost the sense of where we were and forgotten the lessons of childhood. No boy is ever far from a place of wonder; only the man, become an expert, forgets the holiness of his own place. We are going to our places more often now. We can look about and see our past and present lives in the places we have inhabited. We can be alone in that place and see the past rush into the present, and feel the spirits of all those we have known there.

OUR PLACES ARE REAL PLACES AND
THEY ARE UNIQUE TO EACH OF US.

August 24

Let yourself live in something that is already rightfully yours—
your own wild mind.
—NATALIE GOLDBERG

There is a mind we construct, an illusory mind built of convention and fear. It is a powerful mind, useful to society and family because it is easily controlled and endlessly productive. This mind has needs and fears and it is a mighty consumer in service to the demands of both. This mind is myopic, seeing only little bits of its magnificent surroundings. This is a docile mind.

Wild mind is a coyote and a lapdog. It consists of the grass clippings on your front lawn and the baobab tree in distant lands. The sun shines at midnight in wild mind. Wild mind drinks rivers and pisses champagne. Wild mind loves without reservation, collapsing into the other, leaving not a trace. Wild mind is the source of all your creativity and the tool of its expression.

WILD MIND HAS BEEN TOO LONG GONE. SHE IS READY TO BOOGIE.

August 25

When my memory fails, I can renew it by looking deeply at the details of distant times, people, and places. I can heal the present by honoring the past.

🌱 🌱 🌱

DESCRIBE YOUR FATHER AS YOU SAW HIM WHEN YOU WERE A BOY.

August 26

Our authentic self, the spirited man, whispers to us in our silence and tugs on our sleeves when we are losing our balance. It has the ability to go where no one else can follow and to bring us back to center. It speaks to us in the voices of our partners, mentors, and allies. This big self understands that a man's tasks are his greatest gifts and it sees clearly the line between the genuine tasks of one's life and the smaller jobs.

When we are disconnected from the true self, we are in pain. We seek to ease the pain, nowadays, with money, sex, and power but discover that these lead only to greater suffering. We can never be satisfied, and the temptations never end.

Reconnected to the spirit, through community and story-telling, we are able to shake off all that is not who we are. Out unique tasks are seen clearly and our masculine roles, as guardians and poets perhaps, become our garments.

I WILL LOOK CLOSELY AT MY ONE TRUE TASK TODAY.

August 27

The most important thing is to find out what is the most important thing.
—SHUNRYU SUZUKI
(to Edward Espe Brown)

My work day begins early. I meditate, have something to eat, and am at work in my home office by seven in the morning. The room is perfumed by my earthen mug of Grandma's Tummy Mint tea and the last tendrils from the incense stick I lit at 5:30. The cursor on the computer screen blinks, attentively, as light climbs through my dormer windows.

Today I sat on my black folding chair, eyes half-closed, feet firmly on the floor, hands folded, and back straight, pondering what Suzuki Roshi had said to Ed Brown. My mind was dammed. I had nothing to say about this exquisite and impenetrable riddle.

Just then, Willie Alexander, age three and a half today, called for me to come to him, right now! I trotted down the stairs and found him, fuzzy-haired and warm from bed, standing in his bathroom. He showed me, with immense pleasure, the great volume of pee in his toilet.

I OFFER THAT PEE, NOT AS THE MOST IMPORTANT THING, BUT AS A POINTER TO IT.

August 28

God, give us grace to accept with serenity the things that cannot be changed, courage to change the things which should be changed, and the wisdom to distinguish one from the other.
—REINHOLD NIEBUHR

In this original form of a popular prayer, the supplicant asks for *grace* to accept with serenity, rather than asking for a *grant* of serenity, as in the popular form. Serenity here is a byproduct of living gracefully.

There is in every man the desire to control his environment, his family, his life and times. We were "captains of our destinies," we thought. It didn't work, can't work. Many men came to a time of despair, a bottoming out, as our dreamworlds fell apart, shards and remnants drifting away into chaos. We felt we had lost control, only to discover that our most numbing illusion was just this illusion of control.

As we learn to let go of the need to control and, instead, to participate, with full body and mind, in the life of the world, we find that the serenity we had previously demanded had become ours, moment to moment, without striving, in the course of our daily lives.

I WILL TRY TO SPEND THIS DAY TOTALLY OUT OF CONTROL.

August 29

It's easy to be a hero and do good, going around helping people. It's most difficult to just watch them struggle and keep your fingers out of it....
—John Daido Loori

A sure way to get a person to resent you is to make sure that they do everything that they are supposed to do. If your child cannot build a very good model car for the school competition and you help him out by doing it yourself so he (who?) won't feel embarrassed, here is what you have taught him: What he does is not good enough, and that someone will do his work for him.

We want to help others sometimes, because we cannot bear to see the pain they are in. We need to ask ourselves if they can bear the pain. It is their pain. This does not mean that we become passive bystanders. When a child falls in the river, we dive in and pull her out just as we would swim out ourselves, having fallen in. We can do for others only what they cannot do for themselves. Can the child with the imperfect model car, which he made with his own hands, stand the embarrassment? Yes, and far better than he can tolerate the insult of having his work done for him.

IN REACHING OUT TO OTHERS, WE MUST BE SURE WE ARE NOT PUSHING AWAY THEIR HUMANITY.

August 30

Women, it's true, make human beings,
but only men can make men.
—MARGARET MEAD

Go to a daytime meeting of your children's school PTA (by whatever name it is known) and count the number of other fathers there. Look at the names on the lists of the various organizing committees for children-related activities in your school, temple, township, or municipality. How many of them are fathers? When you're at home with the kids, is that called "baby-sitting"?

For most of this century, boys have grown up in the absence of their fathers. The father's place was in the direct service of something other than the family. Men fought the wars. The wars are over for now. Men were the workers. Now the task is often shared.

Now men are the story-tellers at home. Men cook and clean house. Men give the baths. Men are looking at their communities to find a way to help the women whose chore it has been to provide for the children.

Obviously not every man will have a son. Some are blessed solely with girls to raise. This does not mean that these men can't help raise boys. There are countless organizations that need men to help raise men. Some men's groups are sponsoring organizations as an alternative to the Boy Scouts or the athletic teams (the only place where fathers seem to be active).

WHAT CAN A MAN DO TO HELP MAKE MEN?

August 31

A mindful day.

This is a day of mindfulness. What is sought here is not a unique day, standing distinctly apart from all others, but a day when the practice of mindfulness moves into the foreground. Today is a day of enrichment and heightened awareness. Please bring this wonderful practice into every day.

Mindfulness is not an esoteric practice. Being mindful simply means being awake. For men, being mindful can mean the beginning of the end of the social masculine trance and the dismembered life. In mindfulness we become aware of the fullness and flow of our lives, one moment at a time.

The Appendix of this book contains specific directions and suggestions. I encourage you to visit a library or bookstore for additional help in this ancient practice. One excellent book is *Full Catastrophe Living* by Jon Kabat-Zinn, Ph.D. The Vietnamese Buddhist monk Thich Naht Hahn has written dozens of books, many of which concern mindfulness. My personal favorites are *The Miracle of Mindfulness* and *Being Peace*.

This is a beautiful day. Please embrace it fully.

September 1

The twenty-second is the autumnal equinox, the beginning of harvest time. Light and dark are in balance.

This is the Jewish month of Ellul. Rosh Hashanah, the new year, is celebrated, and Yom Kippur, the solemn day of atonement, is observed.

September 2

Vigilance, self knowledge, and discernment: these are the true guides of the soul.
—ABBA POEMAN

We have not been in the habit of guiding our souls. That was an endeavor better left to the parson, the shrink, or an occasional stroll through the self-help section at the mall bookstore (no purchase necessary). We were otherwise occupied.

Perhaps we grew up in a home where the spiritual life was associated with little old blue-haired ladies, smelling faintly of lavender and gin. For some, the life of the spirit seemed entirely too "churchy" and dull. The belief in a higher authority was not for us.

When we woke up to the recognition of what it was that had been making us so uncomfortable for so long, that is, the longing for the spirit, we plunged enthusiastically back into the spiritual mass-market racks, devouring the words of disciplines from Anabaptist to Zen. That eventually collapsed as well, just under the gruesome weight of time and energy.

Having forgiven ourselves for both our blindness and our spiritual avarice, we could proceed to the simple, sweaty task of meditation and contemplation, inner-directed, with or without a teacher. When we engage in this simple practice, every day, we begin to live our own lives, responsibly and passionately.

❦ ❦ ❦

HOW DO I PRACTICE THE SPIRITUAL LIFE TODAY?

September 3

Addiction is any compulsive, habitual behavior that limits the freedom of human desire.
—GERALD G. MAY

Does that mean that a man who loves his work is addicted to it? What about the father who is active, daily, in community affairs, running a scout troop and a softball team? Is he addicted? And if this is addiction, at least it's positive addiction, isn't it?

For the spirited man, no attachment that leads away from his intuitive, compassionate, whole self is tolerable. When his wholeness is deformed by dishonesty with self and others, when his priorities are out of balance, or his willpower weakened, he is in trouble. The addictions—to substances, vocations, entertainment, consumption, people, family, hobbies, sex, or the spiritual life—can do more to neutralize the masculine spirit than any political or social tyranny we could invent.

WITHOUT THE FREEDOM OF AWE AND WONDER WE ARE CRIPPLED WHERE WE STAND.

September 4

... *The glamour of childish days is upon me,*
my manhood is down in the flood of remembrance,
I weep like a child for the past.
—D.H. LAWRENCE

The past is constantly pouring into the present, informing our days and enriching our lives. The present moment contains every scent, every touch, every impression
we have ever encountered. The task is to allow ourselves to
linger with the long-forgotten scenes that come to rest, in-
sistently, with us. It is not necessary, in fact it is violence, to
push aside the tears that rise when we see again, as in this
poem, for example, our mother's feet on the pedal of the
piano. At that moment, we are being handed a piece of our
story. We must be with it for a while and then move on.

🌿 🌿 🌿

WHEN THE PAST "INTRUDES" I WILL WELCOME THE MEMORIES
AS TEACHERS.

September 5

If they're so healthy, there must be something wrong with them.
—KEN B.

When a man has awakened spiritually, the usual experience is that nothing much has changed. As the Zen master says, this awakening is "nothing special." The personality remains just about as it was, still abrasive if once abrasive, introverted if once introverted. We still carry a satchel full of unfinished business and unscratched itches.

This was pretty bewildering to most of us. We wondered who had turned out the great white light. And where were the angels with their trombones, the minor dieties with their capes and scrolls? Fearing we had done it wrong (again), we felt it necessary to play the part of the enlightened one. We dressed in sand-colored linen, wore Birkenstocks and bells—for a short while. This was learned behavior, to act the part to be noticed. Businessman, country squire, jock, or saint, all dumb show. Our sanctimony and costumes yielded to our emergent understanding of the reality of the spiritual jolt we had received. That is, we had roots at last. Our exile was ended and our lives had a center. We had had a change in values rather than a change in costume.

THE EMPEROR DOES HAVE NEW CLOTHES.

September 6

When I begin to think about those I would exclude from my love, I will look hard at the times that I was pushed aside and move, resolutely, to create a greater neighborhood.

WHO ARE YOUR "PEOPLE"? WHAT IS YOUR TRUE COMMUNITY?

September 7

Habit is overcome by habit.
—THOMAS À KEMPIS

Men have bought some interesting packages in service of the yearning for freedom of spirit. We have attended seminars, read books, spent weekends with the gurus of the two-night stand of ecstasy and aura polishing. The rush was terrific and we would emerge into the world on Monday morning, eager to keep feeling the way we did on Sunday night, when we had come out of the woods or left the hotel ballroom. By Thursday, we were scanning the catalogues looking for another intensive high or plundering the bookshelves.

This is, after all, the culture of instant gratification. It's only a matter of time until a God's World franchise opens up in the mall, next to The Gap, just down the hall from the Nature Company, and cheek by jowl with Victoria's Secret.

We know this doesn't work. Daily reaffirmation of change leads to change. We are meeting with other men on a regular basis. We have established personal rituals of meditation and solitude. We live our changes one day at a time. The conscious life is a gift to be protected, daily, not a commodity to be bought and discarded.

THE HABIT OF CHANGE IS HABIT-FORMING.

September 8

What is the secret of the trick
How did I get so old so quick?
—OGDEN NASH

My peers and I are now called "ageing hippies." I spent much of the middle sixties, including the distant "Summer of Love," smack dab in the middle of the Haight Ashbury district of San Francisco. My hair was long, I reeked of Patchouli, and my eyes had a chronic glaze. I never thought about growing old(er).

We wanted to change the world and we wanted to change it "right now". Not much changed.

The gift and the challenge of age is in seeing that those things worth changing will not change in a single lifetime. When that knowledge sinks from the mind to the heart, faith is born.

WHAT WILL MY LEGACY BE?

When I am angry or resentful of someone, I will look more deeply and lovingly at that anger. In there somewhere is a picture of who I am afraid I might really be. I can learn to love that "other."

DRAW A MASK OF YOUR "SHADOW" SELF.

September 10

*Happiness is knowing that you do not necessarily
require happiness.*
—WILLIAM SAROYAN

The aim of life is not to be happy. It is quite possible that happiness will be a by-product of a life consciously lived, but the moment that becomes the goal, it is lost.

We have thought that we could buy happiness. Another VCR blinking 12:00, 12:00, 12:00, 12:00, or another car (trade every three years) or another lover, fading to disappointment over time. We thought, as well, that happiness would be the reward *after* we got a promotion, bought a house, and in general just did as we were told. If we weren't happy, we felt inadequate to the task of living. We had done it wrong somehow. Further, we demanded that those around us be happy. "Are you a happy person?" we asked on the first date. That is, can you pass the culture's primary test of accomplishment? None could. We could not.

We have learned, as spirited men, that even a single life is too immense and too mysterious to be directed toward any mean end. Heading, bullheadedly, toward Happiness, we missed rapture and turned away from grief. Goal-less, we sail before the wind and tend to our souls.

🌿 🌿 🌿

MY HAPPINESS IS NONE OF MY BUSINESS.

September 11

Parents are the bones on which children sharpen their teeth.
—PETER USTINOV

Those of us who are fathers often make a fundamental mistake. We want our children to like us. This seems particularly to be so if we did not like our fathers. It is not our job to be liked and it is not our children's job to like us. We are, rather, the expanding walls of the room they are exploring. We are the performers, not them.

In recent years, our fears have led us to restrict the lives of children, and, buying into pop culture, we have categorized and labeled them. Surrounded by children, we've taken workshops on our "inner child." Indeed, indeed! The pain of letting children make mistakes was so great that we denied them free expression and craziness. It's past time to let kids be crazy again.

When has the school play ever been performed by the parents for the children's delight? When have we ever let the children march down Fifth Avenue while Big Bird, Mickey and Dumbo sat in the bleachers applauding them?

I CAN ALLOW CHILDREN TO BE CHILDREN, NO MATTER HOW CRAZY IT MAKES ME. THAT'S THEIR JOB.

September 12

On a trip on the Ogowe River in 1915 it came to me that reverence for life is the only basis on which a viable ethic can be built.
—ALBERT SCHWEITZER

When the door to the spiritual life is opened you are doomed, because from that moment it will never stay closed. The faint light in the opening haunts your darkest rooms and insinuates itself even beneath your tightly shut eyelids.

When small numbers of men began to connect with each other, outside of the locker room, the barroom, and the boardroom, they—we—began a religious pilgrimage that was unique to each individual, personal but not private. We awoke and, supported by our brothers, were able to shake off the roles and demands of an often demented society and feel, for the first time, what it is to be truly male. In our connection with each other, we began to sense the connection to all the living. We were sensitized, through story and ritual, to the wonder of life. We began to see with our hearts.

TODAY WE CAN LIVE WITH SERENITY IN OUR CONNECTION, RATHER THAN ANXIETY IN THE ILLUSION OF SEPARATION.

September 13

A mindful day.

This is a day of mindfulness. What is sought here is not a unique day, standing distinctly apart from all others, but a day when the practice of mindfulness moves into the foreground. Today is a day of enrichment and heightened awareness. Please bring this wonderful practice into every day.

Mindfulness is not an esoteric practice. Being mindful simply means being awake. For men, being mindful can mean the beginning of the end of the social masculine trance and the dismembered life. In mindfulness we become aware of the fullness and flow of our lives, one moment at a time.

The Appendix of this book contains specific directions and suggestions. I encourage you to visit a library or bookstore for additional help in this ancient practice. One excellent book is *Full Catastrophe Living* by Jon Kabat-Zinn, Ph. D. The Vietnamese Buddhist monk Thich Naht Hahn has written dozens of books, many of which concern mindfulness. My personal favorites are *The Miracle of Mindfulness* and *Being Peace*.

This is a beautiful day. Please embrace it fully.

September 14

I did not attend his funeral, but I wrote a nice letter saying that I approved it.
—Mark Twain

If I found that I was universally liked, I would fall into a suffocating depression, certain in the knowledge that I had failed to make much of a mark. Likewise, if I "liked" everyone, without regard for their ugly little deceits or loathsome hygiene, I would be assured of a particularly toasty little corner of hell.

Does everyone like me? How could they?

September 15

The fundamental defect of fathers is that they want their children to be a credit to them.
—BERTRAND RUSSELL

Our betrayal of our own children is a shame that has been buried deep and denied with conviction. Few of us could admit the embarrassment we felt at the boy who couldn't swing a baseball bat or the girl who could. If we were told that a child of ours was having trouble at school, we seldom stopped to wonder if the school was at fault for not seeing the child in his wholeness. We blamed the child for not getting along.

The pain of our children too often resonated with our own hidden pain, setting off alarms we had not heard since childhood. We said that we didn't want our children to have to suffer through what we had experienced when what we really meant was that we did not want to suffer it again ourselves.

As we have opened ourselves to other men, discovering a common experience of childhood feelings of not being good enough, we have begun to let go of our demands, rarely articulated, that our children not be who they are, but who we must have them be. One of the great rewards of the spirited life is the acceptance of our limits and the knowledge of our uniqueness. We have let ourselves off the hook and forgiven ourselves for our unreasonable expectations.

AS WE HAVE PUT ASIDE OUR MASKS AND MELTED OUR ARMOR,
WE HAVE BECOME ABLE TO
"FORGIVE OTHERS AS WE FORGIVE OURSELVES."

September 16

One time we were repelled and angered, for example, by the sight of a homeless family asleep in a cardboard box in "our" neighborhood. They were failures, we told our children; sad, yes, but look at how grateful we should be not to be like them. We had many shields between us and the reality of the homeless people, poor people, the diseased, the alcoholic or drug-addicted people, the emotionally stunted or mentally ill people. We did not in fact refer to them as "people" at all, only as "the _____."

A miracle of awakening to our full masculine capacity is to see those shields dissolve and to begin to feel within us the heartbeat of the many. We find it impossible, with humility as our guide, to see "the other" in the faces of those around us. Not one of us has become a saint in this period of masculine renewal, and many need to be wary of saintliness, but we have become able to feel the suffering of another as our own.

NOW, IN THE COMPANY OF MEN WHO WILL SHARE OUR PAIN, WE CAN BE GUARDIANS TO THOSE WHO SUFFER.

September 17

If the child is safe everyone is safe.
—G. Campbell Morgan

Men have rediscovered in themselves an empathy and compassion that was unknown to the dejected man of the past. Our productivity can now be measured in more than our ability to make and consume. The way we dress and the kind of wheels we drive don't matter as much as they once did. The priorities are changing. They had to.

We awoke to a world filled with poison or, worse, indifference. The children were being sold violence and death as entertainment. The fathers were no longer the storytellers. The family, however configured, was no longer the vessel for the religious life.

Today we know that keeping "the child" safe means to keep the children safe. We know that, in reality, the children close to us are harmed when we permit any of the children of the earth to be harmed. We know that "our" children can feel the pain of a child they have never seen far more acutely than we can, and that we betray the love of our own when we deny the humanity of the other.

HOW ARE THE CHILDREN DOING TODAY?

September 18

When I am being hard on myself, I will look carefully at my assets and gifts.

DRAW A MASK OF YOUR IDEAL SELF.

September 19

Rock 'n' roll is part of a pest to undermine the morals of the youth. It is sexualistic, unmoralistic.
—NORTH ALABAMA WHITE CITIZENS COUNCIL

Don't expect to find a pious tract on facing adult responsibility, putting aside childish things, and facing the future with dignity here.

I was twelve years old when Elvis Presley made his first record, and I went to the same high school as the Everly Brothers. I knew Little Richard scared my parents and the thought made me happy. When I heard the difference between his version of "Tutti Frutti" and Pat Boone's honkie version I wanted to do something about it. I didn't know what but something clearly had to be done to shut this white man's face and let Little Richard scream. I sometimes watched *American Bandstand*, but I knew that wasn't rock and roll. I listened to WLAC and WSM in Nashville, late at night, singing along with the White Rose Petroleum Jelly ads. I heard Bobby Blue Bland and Muddy Waters and John Lee Hooker. I applauded Jerry Lee Lewis's great balls of fire, and Gene Vincent told me all about woman love.

Rock and roll is supposed to be dangerous, the man says. I've never gotten over it and I hope I never do. It is a pitiful thing to deny to the children the great energy that transformed us as boys.

WHERE DID I LEAVE THOSE ROCK AND ROLL SHOES?

September 20

It is the responsibility of every adult ... to make sure that children hear what we have learned from the lessons of life and to hear over and over that we love them and that they are not alone.
—MARIAN WRIGHT EDELMAN

It is the conceit of every generation that the newer generation has it harder, not easier, than they did. And it has been the task of each passing generation to deny it.

It's true at last, and it takes courage to say so. It ain't easy growing up now. It is genuinely more difficult for children today.

Sex kills. The rain is poisonous. The air suffocates. Although God isn't dead, he is a either a wimp or a gay basher. Some grown people murder children, singly, or in groups with "smart" bombs.

Now a transgenerational group of men is taking the role of guardian, not warrior. We tell the children we love them actively, by refusing to accept the status quo. We are the storytellers and the poets. We guard the hearth. Our work enriches spiritually and materially. We listen rather than speak.

TODAY I CAN LISTEN DEEPLY TO THE SORROW OF THE CHILDREN.

September 21

Success is relative: It is what we can make of the mess we've made of things.
—T. S. Eliot

We make odd demands of ourselves. We keep doing what we've been doing because if we've been doing it, it must be we're supposed to be doing it. We fall to pieces in the process but "a man's gotta' do what a man's gotta' do."

Who said that?

What did we think we were going to win by killing ourselves with work or duty? What was the prize? Sex? Envy? Comfort?

We were fooled and when the drugs wore off, our freedom was a gift given to all beings.

WHAT NOW IS THE MEASURE OF OUR SUCCESS?

September 22

To recover my imagination, I need only recover my story. I will look with great concentration at the smallest details of my places.

DRAW THE FIRST ROOM YOU REMEMBER.

September 23

... we're hard-wired for the paleolithic. We need less technological cleverness, more understanding, more atonement for our violence to creation.
—Wes Jackson

We have been so entranced by the glitter of technology and so seduced by its comfort that we have failed to look hard at the carnage its development has caused. Along the way to instant communication, we lost communion. Technocratic, multinational, corporatized man got way out of balance. The immature masculine replaced wonder with common amazement and awe with mere surprise. In doing violence to creation, we did violence to ourselves.

The mature masculine is connected to the earth and is its champion and its servant. As we develop this long-neglected part of ourselves, the lover/farmer, we are able to put aside the twinkle toys and get dirt between our toes again.

When I am enchanted by technoglitter today, I will look closely at the price tag.

September 24

Men who become nurturant in the family often feel they are "mothering" rather than "fathering."
—ARTHUR AND LIBBY LEE COLMAN

When the mother is home with the children, she is just home with the children. When the father is home with the children, he is "baby-sitting," a subservient and restricted duty, reserved for those who are not deemed capable of or called upon to nurture.

The role of the father has been an impoverished one, wounding the man, the family, and by extension, the whole constellation of living things. The father has been merely the hero, the stern disciplinarian, the visitor from the wider world, and too often, the intruder and the villain. Men now, with their partners where possible, are reinventing the father, casting off the Judeo-Christian father myth, and searching for the capacity to nurture both at home and in the wider world.

This transformation of the father is going to take far longer than the life span of most fathers alive today.

IT'S TIME TO GET STARTED. WE ARE MUTANTS AND MIGHT AS WELL BE GOOD AT IT.

September 25

A father who takes care of his child physically and emotionally is not a mothering father, but a father *pure and simple—he gives reality to a word that until now has remained practically empty of meaning.*
—GUY CORNEAU

I do not father my son *like* my wife mothers him. Instead, by caring for him in response to my own deeper instincts and bone-deep knowledge of what to do, I am initiating him into a world we can explore together—the world of the nurturing man, the spirited one, a place that is dark at times and redolent with deep scents of humus and sweat.

My daughter is too old now to be shown these masculine mysteries by me, or perhaps the world and I were too young in her youth. I would have if I could have. Her generation missed the masculine parent as he is now emerging. My wish for her is that her husband be a spirited man. The generation of men who are fathers now carry a great burden. It is for them—us—to become the earth fathers, consciously connected to the source, radiant in our masculinity, powerful in our love of family and home.

🌿 🌿 🌿

WHEN I'M THE MAN OF THE HOUSE, WHO AM I?

September 26

It is a terrible thing
To be so open; it is as if my heart
Put on a face and walked into the world.
—SYLVIA PLATH

One of the most difficult tasks facing men over the coming years will be to "change in public." Individually and en masse, we have already experienced ridicule and smug criticism, more often it seems from men than from women, of the often faulty, always genuine, attempts to uncover the deep masculine. This is a slow process and in the quick-fix, mall-church culture, some patience is going to be required.

We men have the right to appear ridiculous.

Awakening from a stupor, we are not likely to find our earth legs right away. Some of the crystal and china is going to be broken, and there are liable to be some strange human noises. We who were told to be good, to be big boys and don't cry, are going to have to wail. Our spontaneity is going to rip the fabric.

We are also finding it helpful to confide in other men and to find solace in knowing our imperfection is universal. It's helpful to bless a younger man, or to seek the blessing of an older man. We'll know when our needs aren't being met and will try something other than a stiff upper lip or extended middle finger to express our sorrow.

🌿 🌿 🌿

SHAKING OFF THE CHAINS IS GOING TO RAISE SOME DUST.

September 27

We now imitate the computer. Our deepest image of ourselves becomes man as rational producer, man identified with his mental processes, his brainpower.
—STUART MILLER

Science fiction movies and novels of the '50s commonly featured alien creatures with enormous, blue-veined heads on skinny necks erect on atrophied bodies, the legs unnecessary and other sensual functions reduced to the critical minimum. These critters were always male, always superior, always possessed of great intellect (thence the enormous craniums to contain these melon-sized organs) and always without feelings.

Their palaces or transportation modules were gleaming and spotless, just like Momma's kitchen. Their gardens, if they used them, were perfectly tended, the plants hybrid, pests and fungus banished.

They often served a higher power, disembodied and envied for it, which held the power to elevate or annihilate at will.

They did not, we assume, screw, and seemed content to consume artificial nutrients in the form of pastes, pills, and powders.

Look closer with your mind's eyes.

Don't they look like babies, too?

I CAN BE ALERT FOR THE INFANTALIZED MASCULINE TODAY.

September 28

Sanity is a madness put to good uses;
waking life is a dream controlled.
—GEORGE SANTAYANA

It is easy to argue that men have gone insane if sanity is simply being in touch with and acting out of one's true nature; one's unique masculine soul. So it's going to take a little craziness to get sane. We are learning to be gently dangerous as we rediscover the mature masculine.

Rather than *"re*covering" we are uncovering the masculine soul. We must not be so concerned with overcoming what we see as defective in ourselves as with embracing these so-called defects as markers of the far borders of our resplendent selves.

We are not focused on fixing our lives and finding salvation. We are deeply involved in paying attention to its complexity and wonder.

🌿 🌿 🌿

LIGHTEN UP!

September 29

The father's thankless position in the family is to be everybody's breadwinner, everybody's enemy.
—J. A. STRINDBERG

We have to empathize with our fathers to heal the father wound. Some of us were taught that our fathers were inadequate and weak. Our mothers criticized them or indulged in general male-bashing. The women's movement often served to aggravate this lie, as men, eager to dismantle patriarchy, joined with those who confuse patriarchy with gender.

Others of us idolized our fathers. Pop on a pedestal. He was the man who conquered the world and, like Odysseus, returned home only to leave again, tearing whole pieces out of his son's heart as he went. In this situation we need to see, as Telemachus did, that our fathers suffered as well.

❧ ❧ ❧

LEARN YOUR FATHER'S STORY. WHAT IS THE STORY THE OLD MAN LIVED? WHO WERE HIS PEOPLE? WHERE WAS HIS REAL HOME? WHERE DID HE COME FROM? WHAT DID HE BELIEVE? WHAT WERE HIS DEMONS? WHO WERE HIS HEROES?

September 30

The worst of a modern stylish mansion
is that it has no place for ghosts.
—OLIVER WENDELL HOLMES

A man's home is his character witness.

In the years of enchantment, we decorated our homes according to fashion. "Masters of the Universe" and wannabes created showplaces of folly and vanity. In the time of soul freedom we live in our homes, learning from them, watching them evolve like the great cathedrals of older times. There are stories in hidden places and in open rooms.

Driven by dissatisfaction and longing to be elsewhere, some would spend more money to make a home look like a farm than it would cost to buy the real thing. We made the taste-makers rich and exhausted our souls.

Now our homes can reflect and invigorate our inner lives. One room might be left empty while another is crammed with books and papers and mismatched chairs, gathered in our journey. There are rich odors of cooking and living, of sex and sweat and play. There are unfinished places and places of rest. There are private places in public. There is serenity in chaos—visible to the heart's eye.

WHAT GHOSTS LURK IN MY HOME, JUST OUT OF SIGHT, READY TO
TELL THEIR STORIES WHEN INVOKED?

October 1

On the fourth of this month is the feast of Saint Francis of Assisi and on the thirty-first is Samhain, All Hallow's Eve, or Halloween. October is also the month of Sukkot, also known as the Jewish feast of tabernacles, the ancient seasonal celebration of gathering of summer crops. It is also the month of Durga Puja, the Indian festival of the Divine Mother, which celebrates the creative feminine force in the universe.

During this month, the gates to the interior open. The harvest is in, the seeds are planted, and the fields are empty. It's the beginning of a time of subtle change and growth that will become chaotic and rich, scented with life, once again, come spring.

This month can be one of simplicity and trust in the eternal processes of life and death.

October 2

The nurse of full-grown souls is solitude.
—JAMES RUSSELL LOWELL

The soulful man does not retreat from the world when he goes into solitude. Rather, in solitude, he enters the world more fully. The distractions and gadgets of modernism are left behind so that the ageless world, alive in the very moment, can be known.

A man needs a place to go to be himself, every day. This can be a room of his own, or it can be a black cushion in a corner of a common room. In this sacred space, he needs his personal religious relics about him. That is, he needs the photos of his grandparents or the cross he wore at first communion. He needs daily contact with the knife his father gave him or the alabaster egg his daughter put in his briefcase as a surprise. He needs to be reconnected, in a concrete way, with the stories of his life.

In this place, the soul can come out to express its needs.

DO I HAVE A DESIGNATED PLACE FOR SOUL CARE?

October 3

When I am gardening I do not think of anything at all; I am wholly involved in the physical work and when I go in, I feel whole again, centered.
—MAY SARTON

As "postmodern" men, we live in a world of frightening complexity and have not yet developed the capacity to deal with it, in most cases. Indeed, we are not certain if learning to live with complexity is a virtue or a curse. It is neither; it is a necessity that can be converted into a blessing. In a sense, it is necessary to create complexity in order to live with it. We deal with our work, our families, our communities, our good works and struggle to keep all these in balance. Until recently we have not found time to forget ourselves. We must steal that time.

Working in the garden, even the most frivolous or commonplace one, is an activity in self-forgetting. A city window box, planted with hot peppers, is a forty-acre farm for the soul of an overworked man. The Convent Men's Group is working on a community garden as an alternative to the crowded and excluding baseball fields. There are many ways to garden and to do so without resorting to metaphor.

PLANT A SEED TODAY.

October 4

The real breakthrough comes when you accept
ownership of your life.
—ALLEN GROSSMAN

We used to say that a man's got to do what a man's got to do, a statement loaded with the implication either of a man fitting into a predetermined role, stoically and with a small measure of ironic contempt, or of the captain of his fate and master of his destiny pursuing some illusory goal with, at best, a grudging but impotent acknowledgment of the needs of others.

These two cartoon roles are being replaced by the gut-deep knowledge of the uniquely human in each of us. As we do the work of awakening the masculine spirit, we encounter no one other than our unique selves, and as we do the conscious work of "soul-making," we see the deep connecting bonds between us and others.

In knowing the connection we have with others, we begin to feel our connection to a power beyond our understanding. The desire to know that power better leads, inevitably, to a spiritual refocusing. At this point, humility and clarity begin to replace vanity and ignorance and we see, often only for a few moments, the reality of the path behind us and ahead of us and know, without doubt, that it is ours.

WHO'S IN CHARGE HERE?

October 5

Sickness is felt, but health not at all.
—Thomas Fuller

James Hillman has pointed out that we have lived for decades in a psychologized society and that things have only gotten worse—crazier, more violent, sadder. This is not to say that this deeply troubled society is a result of the psychologization, only that personal and social healing needs to come from some deeper place.

The awakened man, learning his own story while hearing the stories of other men, and of his family and partners, is unearthing that deeper place and is learning to nurture it. Healing is happening in the community, rather than the therapist's office. Open hearts open doors that no amount of "head shrinking" can see.

The healing of the man takes place in the healing of his environment.

October 6

The winter solstice is approaching. Today I planted daffodil bulbs, surprised by early snow.

They are tucked up against the porch of my house, in a small plot which gets plenty of sun. I suspect I will know they are there, all through the winter, still a few months off.

I am learning, with my brothers, to see the spiritual in the ordinary.

October 7

My religion is very simple—my religion is kindness.
—HH THE DALAI LAMA

One day lived with kindness as the primary motivator in every action taken, every connection made would probably be a day of great awakening for most of us. Imagine, for example, not getting angry today at people who drive carelessly or not getting frustrated with children who are noisy and childlike. Imagine a day of being kind to those who are seen as competitors, whether in business or in the rush for the closing elevator door. Imagine telling your partner how much you admire something she has done or noticing the efforts made by a co-worker. Imagine telling your child a story, pulled from the depths of your imaginings, rather than subjecting her to a night of television or solitary reading. Imagine small anonymous kindnesses like picking up candy wrappers from the sidewalk. Imagine larger kindness, like saying no to anything your government might do that harms or kills. Imagine saying no with kindness.

IMAGINE BEING KIND TO YOURSELF AS THE STARTING PLACE FOR THIS DAY OF KINDNESS. AND DO IT.

October 8

I realize the comfort of self-involvement and will turn resolutely from it to share my life, purposefully and without hope.

October 9

I married a person, at last, who was not my type. Our differences are irreconcilable, and our conflicts like the head-on collisions of diesel locomotives. At times I am silk and she is steel. I am reasonable, she is out of control; or, I am rigid and she is spontaneous. There are days when I think I could willingly murder, bury, and dance on the grave of the spiteful bitch. There are other days, happily more frequent, when no words I speak can surround my feelings of connection to her. I feel blessed by the inadvertent touch of her hand on mine beneath the blankets, and when I look at our son, I am mystified by the magic she carries.

I am greater than I was before I married her, and less. This partnership continues to reveal to me elements of myself, a useful and frightening passivity, for example, that I never saw, and it dissolves fantasies about myself (my uniqueness is one) that were killing my heart.

When the romantic illusion evaporated and we we finally stepped into the ring, pulled the gloves on, and set out to defend ourselves, we stopped fighting.

DO I HAVE THE COURAGE TO STAY FULLY IN MY MARRIAGE?

October 10

When you love someone all your saved-up
wishes start coming out.
—Elizabeth Bowen

Here is the first thing to know about falling in love. We don't decide to do it. No matter what we think, no matter how practical or wise we might consider ourselves to be, most of us fall into this "sacred catastrophe" at the most unexpected moments. Conjugal love arrives, proclaimed by angels and demons, fully prepared to enlighten us if we let it.

This has been a terrifying promise for most men for a long while. And little wonder. No, we weren't ready. We had lost the way to the altar. We had become adults without spiritual initiation and had had to live without loving mentors. We received increasingly universalized and frivolous instruction in the art of marriage from a culture determined to be productive rather than soulful. Our curriculums did not include Love 101, or Devotion and Surrender (graduate students only).

Love between a man and a woman is too complex to be left to books and experts. Don't look here for how to love your wife. Look to your heart first and then to the community you are building. There is readiness in community that can be transmitted to the timid one—each of us, that is, who is moving toward the awful gift of love.

FALLING INTO LOVE IS A DAILY TRIP.

October 11

The only right love is that between couples
whose passion leads them both, one through the other,
to a higher possession of their being.
—Pierre Teilhard de Chardin

Love is possession. Love is another name for dependence or domination. Love is a trick to ensure propogation. Love is only sexual. Love is only spiritual. Love is a myth of "dysfunction." Love is gentle, love is kind. Love is tyranny. Love is an addiction. Love is a myth. Love is a mystery.

❧ ❧ ❧

My feelings of love are not for analysis.
There's so little time.

October 12

Life always gets harder toward the summit—the cold increases, responsibility increases.
—Friedrich Nietzsche

     The soft man, abandoned by the father and redeemed by the corporate consumer culture, fantasizes an easy chair on the summit. The illusion that led us said that we would someday step aside for the younger generation, as if our work was completed when we passed a socially designated "camp five."

     To the contrary, the soulful man sees that it is the responsibility of the younger men to honor those closer to the summit, not to betray them, just as it is the responsibility of the higher climbers to mark the path—to trailblaze. Let's not get lost in the metaphor here. The truth is a simple one: We never retire.

🌳 🌳 🌳

THE ACHIEVEMENT OF THE SPIRITED LIFE IS NOT SLOTH BUT VIGOR.

October 13

Restfullness is a quality for cattle; the virtues are all active, life is alert.
—ROBERT LOUIS STEVENSON

For decades, men have bought the yarn of contentment and repose as the reward for a life well lived. For "well lived" read overworked, burdened with material goods, alienated, and depressed. The mantra of *produce/consume/rest* has lurked in our breathing, so delicate and so emphatic that we never noticed it. We have been eaten alive by the illusion of the rest to come.

A reality of the spirited and mindful life is to see that distant mirage evaporate. The authentic masculine is restless and inquisitive, and men and society have suffered as this male spirit has been surpressed.

Personal and cultural change demand involvement and sacrifice, not in the old patriarchal ways, which assumed the offering of a man's body in war or his spirit in providing the merely frivolous, but in older ways yet, which encourage selflessness and community, chivalry and simple kindness.

HAVE I CONFUSED TAKING IT EASY WITH PASSIVITY AND FRIGHT?

October 14

Many men [at midlife—ed.] remain stuck in a shaky myth of their own power, alienated from the rest of themselves.
—SAMUEL OSHERSON

We men can so easily find ourselves stuck in the corner of the chessboard, crown firmly in place, surveying all the furious motion in front of us, and horrified in the unspoken knowledge of our vulnerability and infirmity. We run a great risk of being thronebound finally, patrician, dismembered and immobile, fully exposed to the sinister wind.

We have been encouraged into being scapegoats by the myth of the warrior and the king. We sit, power-filled, at the head of the table, whether in the dining room or the boardroom, while our souls yearn for the freedom of powerlessness.

The choice to take the path of soul-caring or to stay on the path of patriarchal power is vivid now and in a way that it has not been for many generations. It is still not the popular choice and it is a damned difficult one, loaded with conflict and obstructions. It exacts humility and honesty. It offers authenticity.

IF I FEEL I'M GETTING STUCK, I'LL JUST MOVE A LITTLE.

October 15

Nature, in giving tears to man, confessed that he
Had a tender heart: this is our noblest quality.
—JUVENAL

A man is never more lovable and more loving than when his great tenderness is manifest in his living. This male tenderness is active and robust; it is not the stuff of sentiment. There is pain in the tender-hearted way. The tender-hearted male is exposed and often scraped raw. The tender-hearted man is a creature of awe and bliss and wonder.

After years of denying our feelings, we fragmented ourselves. We became many different parts of a man, unincorporated, cleaved into mute pieces, disheartened. We were the abandoners of ourselves. Our tender hearts disappeared beneath the thickening dust of our dismemberment.

Just as I was leaving the noise and mixed energies of a farewell party for my friend Mark before he left for a year in Florence, he pulled himself away from a telephone call and the crowd of busy friends to say "I love you" to me.

We are two men whose hearts are sweeter for that instinctive, illuminating instant.

TODAY, IN THE PROCESS OF OPENING UP OUR HEARTS TO THE
HEARTS OF OTHERS, WE ARE REGAINING OUR HUMANITY AND
HEALING OUR EARLY WOUNDS.

October 16

I will cultivate the habit of looking outside of my usual narrow range of concerns and learn to share deeply with another man.

CALL A MALE FRIEND. TALK ABOUT ANYTHING BUT MONEY, SEX, OR POWER.

October 17

A mindful day.

This is a day of mindfulness. What is sought here is not a unique day, standing distinctly apart from all others, but a day when the practice of mindfulness moves into the foreground. Today is a day of enrichment and heightened awareness. Please bring this wonderful practice into every day.

Mindfulness is not an esoteric practice. Being mindful simply means being awake. For men, being mindful can mean the beginning of the end of the social masculine trance and the dismembered life. In mindfulness we become aware of the fullness and flow of our lives, one moment at a time.

The Appendix of this book contains specific directions and suggestions. I encourage you to visit a library or bookstore for additional help in this ancient practice. One excellent book is *Full Catastrophe Living* by Jon Kabat-Zinn, Ph.D. The Vietnamese Buddhist monk Thich Naht Hahn has written dozens of books, many of which concern mindfulness. My personal favorites are *The Miracle of Mindfulness* and *Being Peace*.

This is a beautiful day. Please embrace it fully.

October 18

> *Parents have become so convinced that educators*
> *know what is best for children that they forget that*
> *they themselves are really the experts.*
> —MARIAN WRIGHT EDELMAN

One of the fruits of the reclaimed masculine is a deep involvement in the true education of our children. We have become sensitive to what they learn from us and, in healing ourselves, we are able to teach them well. We know that our children value our teachings and we are able to give them with a clarity that is new and exciting to us. We know that our children are not fooled by our attempts to buy them and that they see through our posturings and self-importance.

Schools and other institutions responsible to our children are learning that there is a new masculine energy that will not tolerate being patronized and that is creating new roles for men. Men are involved in schools now in new ways; the Little League coach is sharing open space with the community gardener.

WHEN WE HONOR THE DEEP MASCULINE, WE CAN CARRY
TEACHINGS TO OUR CHILDREN.

October 19

Children need models rather than critics.
—JOSEPH JOUBERT

Who decided that men, mainly, who happen to be good at sports should be given the job of mentor if they don't ask for it? Charles Barkley, for example, is a hell of a basketball player but I wouldn't want him to raise my kids. I admire him far more for his clear desire not to have the job than any of the misguided jocks who plague the airways with their barely literate, adenoidal injunctions to just "say no" or "finish school" or whatever else happens to be the chic way out of parental responsibility this season.

Let's take some of our children's attention back from the overpaid athletes and the TV comic book heroes. Not all the attention needs to be diverted; the jocks and clowns are mythic creatures and sometimes tell the ancient stories. But the father's teachings are the ones that can penetrate to the heart of a child. We teach them at every moment. Our stories inform their lives and we tell them ceaselessly.

WHO IS TELLING YOUR CHILDREN STORIES TONIGHT? WHO IS CARRYING THE MASCULINE TEACHINGS TONIGHT?

October 20

A religious awakening which does not awaken the sleeper to love has roused him in vain.

—JESSAMYN WEST

There is great abundance in the "sacred catastrophe" of breakdown and awakening. We are given gifts of sight and hearing, of smell, and of touch and taste. We begin to sense the sacred in our daily lives and to appreciate the depth of simple ritual, such as watering plants or praying.

The awakening to love is immediate, but it is often brutally confronted by the old soft masculine; the corrupt boy is frightened by this new and tender heart. We want to turn away because loving means pain.

Love treats love in this time of fearfulness. We can love our fears as part of us. "This too, this too" becomes the great mantra of acceptance and the opening of love to love.

LOVE LEADS THE WAY TO LOVE.

October 21

When I look closely at the chapters of my life, I see that at no time was I alone. I will recall the company I have kept in the most dramatic and most mundane of moments.

WRITE ABOUT THE GREATEST CHALLENGE YOU HAVE FACED.

October 22

And if you say that I am young and tender, and that the time for seeking is not come, you ought to know that to seek true religion, there is never a time not fit....

—Prince Siddhartha
(via Jack Kerouac)

The experience of religion has been fragmentary and confusing for men in the economic era. Our young souls were wildly curious about gods and devils. We were in awe of the long night sky and the depths of oceans and lakes. We regarded death coolly, with small breaths moving gently. We felt moments of belonging, with moms or dads or friends, that were charged with bewildered joy. There were times of rage and sorrow when we dumbly questioned our estrangement and the uncertainty of every moment.

Our questions were religious ones, but we were given the tepid answers of mere science or psychology. We were unkempt theologians.

We learned the religion of our family and our peers. We saw where they worshiped—Dad at the office, Mom in the car—and we accepted this anemic reality, reluctantly, as our own. These questions never vanished. Now, in the company of other men, they are being coaxed to the surface again and are suffusing our lives with awe and vigor. We are charged with honoring our own inquiries and with seeing them mirrored in the deep questioning of our children.

OUR OBLIGATION IS TO SEE THE SACRED THAT IS HIDDEN
IN THE ORDINARY AND TO BLESS OUR QUESTIONS
AND THE QUESTIONS WE ARE ASKED.

October 23

"... This too, this too" was the main meditation instruction....
Through these few words we were encouraged to soften and open
to see whatever we encountered, accepting the truth with a wise
and understanding heart.
—JACK KORNFIELD

Men are taught that they are the captains of their fates and the masters of their souls. Or is it the other way around? We are taught that willpower and grit will give us control over people and circumstances. If we are strong enough and willful enough, if we are warriors in business and in bed, then the world will reward us with wealth and power. Control is everything.

The feeling of failure when it doesn't come off as planned goes deep. We are ashamed because we are less than men, or bitter because of the evil hand we have been dealt. The greater the resistance of the world to our plans for it, the greater effort we made and the weaker and more discouraged we became. Our mantra was "not this, not this." We became tougher and more bruised. We gave away big chunks of ourselves to maintain the illusion of control.

Finally, breathless with the effort at control, we gave it up. Our families would have to go ahead and fail, the country would have to go to the dogs and the world would have to burn to a cinder. We could do no more to save any of them. We began, often with "fear and loathing," to accept things, positive or negative, just as they were.

They got better.

TODAY WHEN I LOSE CONTROL, I'LL JUST LET IT GO.

October 24

When we were just putting in time between birth and death, we were desensitized to all the messages we received from the social and political environment. We lost the ability to question. Numbed, we became dumb. We absorbed the messages of greed and self-centeredness passively and then acted on them, tempered only by lack of time or money, but seldom by ethics or, more properly, horror. We wittingly called ourselves "consumers," pridefully demanding the rights due to such a being. We became bored and weary and secretly ashamed of our selfishness and our complicity.

The spirited man seeks to find his connection to his "inner consumer," to become conscious in order to lovingly distance himself from this tedious wraith, and at the same time to strengthen his connection to his fellows. Through the discovery of his deeper desires, for simplicity and harmony, he has discovered his humanity and has awakened the healer in, and of, his soul.

TODAY, WHEN I AM TEMPTED TO SERVE MYSELF,
I WILL RESOLUTELY FIND SOMEONE TO SERVE.

Nobody today is normal, everybody is a little bit crazy or unbalanced, people's minds are running all the time. . . . They are eaten alive by their egos.
—TAISEN DESHIMARU

Consider what we call normal today. It is normal to be marginally exhausted much of the time, to live in a state of uncertainty about our jobs, our relationships, our security, and our pasts and futures. A normal marriage is a silently negotiated agreement not to touch each other in a way that might engage the spirit. It is normal to agree that the schools, run by strangers, know better than we how to teach our children, and that public "role models" are important to anyone other than sports shoe manufacturers. We say that violence and brutality, whether in mindless wars or in our children's entertainment, are just a normal part of growing up. In the search for more comfort and less confusion, we attempt to control or deny the complex rhythms of the natural world. At the end of it all, death finds us unfulfilled and fearful.

There is a way out of this ego-driven madness. Men are giving a new definition to normal these days, not because of any great virtue but because of a soul-fatigue that forced us to rebel against this inner violence of sluggishness and isolation. We got weary of being weary.

EXHAUSTED BY BEING SO COMFORTABLE, WE ARE BECOMING INVIGORATED BY RESTLESSNESS.

October 26

Put your heart, mind, intellect and soul even to your smallest acts. This is the secret of success.
—SWAMI SIVANANDA

Imagine a private time standing or sitting beneath a cascade of temperate water, your body caressed and cleansed in a perfumed atmosphere, every sense alive to the very moment with no thought of past or future.

Or think about the morning shower before rushing off to somewhere else.

Consumed by doing what we thought we had to do, we became numb to what was all about us. We missed the taste of apples or grilled fish, the texture of a lover's skin, or the surreal phantoms at play in a resting mind while we were having a quick lunch, grabbing a quick rut, or taking a quick nap.

In awakening to a spirited life, we have been overwhelmed by the exquisite pleasures of the ordinary. The practice of conscious living brings us closer to our world, our families, and our deepest sources of power and riches.

I WILL SENSE THE TRUE SPEED OF MY LIFE TODAY.
WHAT AM I MISSING?

October 27

Tom Seaver: Hey, Yogi, what time is it?
Yogi Berra: You mean now?
—JON WINOKUR
Zen To Go

This impenetrable exchange is offered as a reminder of the divine right to be impossible.

Such wonderful madness can cause an eruption of laughter that drown the mullings of the intellect and challenge the gods of reason.

When we become too solemn, we are stuck in the glue, going nowhere. Perhaps it's time to enjoy the view.

HEY YOU, WHAT TIME IS IT?

October 28

By the time we have awakened to our spirited masculinity, most of us have put aside our anger at our parents or at whatever furies we imagined had so narcotized us to our true and splendid masculine selves. We have settled our accounts and let the bad guys off the hook. We've gotten involved in the reality of our expanding lives and begun to confront the other unacceptable definitions of who we are assumed to be. The marketers and advertisers know that our place of worship is not the mall any longer and the holy books we browse through don't arrive unbidden and fourth class, and they are starting to panic.

To borrow out of context from the Buddhists, it is "no small matter" to be in touch with our souls. We are responsible, that is, we are able to respond, to the needs of the planet in a grand sense and concurrently to the needs of those who depend on us. Our children, whoever they are and wherever they show up, see whole men now, dependable and humble.

MY NEEDS ARE SIMPLER, MY DESIRES FEW. I CAN FEEL THE POWER
OF MOVING IN THE SPIRITUAL REALM.

October 29

Nature is what she is—amoral and persistent.
—STEPHEN JAY GOULD

The spirited man is not able to sentimentalize nature. His lawn probably isn't very neat and he isn't likely to admire theme parks or recreational vehicles. He hikes slowly in the mountains rather than rushing to the peak. He enters the forest consciously and with awe. He doesn't take many toys to the beach, but swims joyously in the supporting water. He understands, with fear and gratitude, the folly of trying to control the natural world. His air conditioner is unplugged most of the time.

✹ ✹ ✹

THE RAIN IN ITS TIME IS WONDERFUL. THE STORM DRIVES ME
AWE-FILLED TO SHELTER.

October 30

When I begin to see my troubles as too dark and my life as too dreary, I will deal with my problems by dealing with problems so much darker than my own. I will enter directly into the process of blessing another.

October 31

As I become aware of my unconscious addictions, I see the barriers that I must pass through on the way to the spirited masculine.

DO NOT BUY ANYTHING TODAY THAT IS NOT CRUCIAL TO YOUR SURVIVAL.

November 1

The first of November is All Saints' Day, or All Hallowmas, a day to honor all martyrs and saints, which probably succeeded a pagan festival of the dead. In the Catholic tradition, November second is All Souls' Day, a day of intercession for the souls of all the dead. This also appears to be an adaptation of festivals in many cultures to honor the dead.

This month we can consciously honor the ancestors in our prayers and stories.

You don't need Little League. You don't even need nine kids.
Four is plenty. . . . If kids want to do something, they'll do
it. They don't need adults to do it for them.
—YOGI BERRA

Patriarchy has found some clever ways to make sure that the children are under control. The dunce cap and stool in the corner was a good one. Boys Scouts and Little League are even better, because they don't even look like punishment. A generation of men, raised on organized fun, are uncovering a spontaneity that delights their hearts and is making them the wisest of parents and leaders. Ours is the radical chore of letting kids be kids. It probably won't happen right away. It is too difficult right now and the world is still a horrid place for many children. If we follow our hearts, we can hope that our daughters' grandchildren will "go out and play" at dusk, without a cadre of anxious and frightened men telling them how to do it.

🌱 🌱 🌱

THE SKILLS TAUGHT BY THE GENERATION OF RE-MEMBERED MEN
ARE THE ABILITY TO BE HONEST AND OPEN AND TO INCLUDE
RATHER THAN EXPEL.

November 3

Imagination is more important than knowledge.
—ALBERT EINSTEIN

Men lost the power of imagination in the process of becoming useful too soon. We were put in uniforms, of baseball or Boy Scouts, at a very early age, and lost the bright and idiosyncratic colors of our blooming individuality. We stopped learning to draw at exactly the point that someone told us that "houses [or airplanes or backyard hoes or dogs] don't look like *that!*" We knew that the sun and the moon were always in the sky at the same time but lost our knowing of such a great sky when we heard patronizing laughter.

Now we see, through our own awakening, that the children are only marginally served by any teachers, wherever they find them, who only know a great deal, because they are denied all the questions. Just so, computers are finally of little use because all they have are answers.

Men today who are committed to getting the real job done are likely to tell a story about themselves, in all their fallibility and uncertainty, or one about the radiator that cooked popcorn for the mice each Friday night, rather than read from a book or "share" TV-watching time.

I AM LEARNING TO SHARE MY WONDER RATHER THAN MY
PEDAGOGY OR ADDICTIONS.

November 4

*Sentimentality is the emotional promiscuity of those
who have no sentiment.*
—NORMAN MAILER

In men's groups or in private talks with another man, we are beginning to regain access to our feelings, long buried by selfishness and isolation. The isolated man could weep, pitiably, in the sanctuary of the darkened theater, or on hearing a particular piece of music, often grandiose or martial. We allowed our emotions full expression in the presence of the impersonal, but were unable to experience the complex and often painful love of another man or woman. We loved our undemanding dogs and abandoned our children when their pain was too great for *us* to bear.

It is a long and difficult road back to sensitivity and empathy. Through connecting with other men and taking responsibility for our lives, we are learning that the soulful man has great power while the isolated man is weak and foolish. I am haunted by the image of Al Pacino as the godfather sitting on the lawn of his great house, alone and cold, just putting in time.

MY TRUE FEELINGS ARE NOT LETHAL.

November 5

Lost in the carnival, noises and blinking lights luring me to sleep, I lose track of my deeper happiness and my greater desire. I will look within, resolutely, when I am getting lost, to find my way.

WHAT IS YOUR DESTINY?

November 6

More wisdom is latent in things-as-they-are than in all the words men use.
—SAINT-EXUPÉRY

The way of little effort is a foreign one to most of us. It seems unmanly to simply move aside when attacked. We became accustomed to force and strength as a way of learning, working, loving, and playing. In tasks as simple as making a bed or as complex as healing the earth, we tried to force compliance rather than sensing the direction of things and cooperating with that. Our beds ended up looking like combat zones and the earth became one.

When we were faced with family, personal, or behavioral problems, we tried to conquer them with our willpower and succeeded only in making them stronger. Many men have dealt with their lives as warriors; this was the pervasive masculine metaphor that nearly killed us. We were somehow at war with the world and rarely noticed that we always lost. We were in outright assault most of the time and we wondered why there was such resistance.

When we begin to align ourselves to the power of "what is" rather than insisting on the illusion of "what should be," we come into harmony with our fellows and with our higher power—at the same moment. Now we can learn to practice effortlessness and harmony rather than war and conflict. That is, we can practice reality rather than illusion.

I WILL EXPEND AS LITTLE EFFORT TODAY AS POSSIBLE.

November 7

When the world has the Way, ambling horses are retired to fertilize fields. When the world lacks the Way, war horses are reared in the suburbs.
—LAO TZU

There is great sorrow in the world, and men, at last, are feeling it. Sensitized by our work with other men, we have broken down the walls of denial and isolation and have let the world in. We are beginning to experience the reality of our connections rather than the illusion of our separation.

It is not easy to play by the new rules, in part because we are not yet sure what they are, but we are no longer content to play the old roles of warrior and conqueror. We have learned to love the whole of life by sharing our secrets and to lead by finding our true masculine power.

I END WAR BY HEALING THE WARRIOR WITHIN.

November 8

. . . if anybody is going to be liberated, it's men who must be liberated in this country.
—Barbara Jordan

The socialization of men by the self-perpetuating patriarchy has led us to a position we have found, finally, to be intolerable. Men by the tens of thousands are saying that we will not fight the wars anymore, but we will bring our masculine love and energy to full heat to put an end to them. We will no longer be reduced to the position of economic animals, suitable only to produce and consume, rewarded with toys and money, but we will work hard to produce a spiritual basis for our lives. We say that we will not be kept from our children by anything and we will not give the raising of our children to anyone; we will only share it—by choice, not by economic/social coercion.

A man's liberation is from his isolation and anxiety. A man's liberation is from the tyranny of his own illusions and ignorance, whatever the source.

I WILL LOOK CLOSELY TO SEE THE BARS THAT SURROUND ME.

November 9

Man qua *thinker may delight in the intricacies of psychology,
but man* qua *lover has not learned to feel in its terms.*
—JOSEPH WOOD KRUTCH

The rational man offers important gifts to his family,
his community, and his world. Ideas, logically pursued and
creatively applied, are of great significance and we do ourselves harm in demeaning this capacity. Men are also admitting that while the head works well, the heart needs
help.

For so long we took pride and comfort in our harmony with family and earth so that when we were installed in the machine of industry, ripped away from our
humble tasks, we suffered so awfully that we built cages
around our feelings.

NOW WE ARE REGAINING OUR FULL EMOTIONAL, EROTIC, AND
SPIRITUAL SELVES, FEELING WITH THE BODY, MIND, AND SPIRIT
AND CULTIVATING OUR WHOLENESS.

November 10

If you wonder whether certain behavior constitutes infidelity I recommend that you ask your spouse.
—Frank Pittman

Our moral compasses are hard-wired from the git-go. Keeping them trained on true north requires only simple daily maintenance. But when it comes to what to do with his pecker, the disspirited man goes haywire. Hugh O'Haire says that when the average guy is horny, he will do just about anything but turn to the person next to him in bed, particularly if she's been there for a while.

We have caused great pain by the acting out of our sexual fantasies or our sexual anger. We have justified behaviors that are harmful and have avoided behaving humbly and openly.

The work to be done is difficult. Many men have thought that philandery is normal behavior, denying its victimizing of both their "lovers" and themselves. As the illusion of power evaporates, he sees the pain he has caused but also feels his own pain for the first time. Right there is where the healing begins.

TODAY WHEN I AM TROUBLED WITH THOUGHTS OF EASY SEX, I WILL SAY "NO THANKS, I'VE HAD ENOUGH."

November 11

Seldom, or perhaps never, does a marriage develop into an individual relationship smoothly and without crises; there is no coming to consciousness without pain.
—CARL GUSTAV JUNG

Many men have run from honest, loving, committed relationships with women because they were certain they would be devoured. To enter the door of true marriage, after falling out of love-bliss, requires the ability to confront every bit of the maleness that was denied by the groom on his long journey to the altar.

As we work toward our wholeness as men, we discover the playful and erotic healing that has been submerged by our drive for power and control. We uncover great pieces of our lost selves in the hearts of our lovers, not in their approval of us, but in their own sacred selves. Our isolation bred deception. Our reunion brings respect.

❦ ❦ ❦

MY "IRRECONCILABLE DIFFERENCES" WITH MY PARTNER MAKE ALL THE DIFFERENCE.

November 12

There are only about twenty murders a year in London and not all are serious—some are just husbands killing their wives.
—A Scotland Yard commander in 1954

Some men's groups show porno movies, slapstick comedies, or fight films for discussion. The degree of honesty reached is often remarkable, as the men go deeper into their feelings. I know men, myself included, who have admitted to the shame they have felt at being repelled by the Marx Brothers or the Three Stooges when all their peers seemed to like them. Other men, also on deep examination, say they are excited by pornography but feel guilt there as well.

What about the statement above? Talk with yourself about it, and then with a male friend, and then with a lover.

🌳 🌳 🌳

HOW MUCH VIOLENCE HAVE I TOLERATED WHEN I KNEW, LOOKING DEEPLY, THAT I WAS REPELLED BY IT?

November 13

Mindful of my responsibility for my personal environment, I will not seek to blame anyone for the mess it's in. I will take care.

DISPOSE OF ANY LITTER YOU SEE.

Defeat means to defeat the mind of contention
that we harbor within.
—MORIHEI UESHIBA

"It" isn't personal.

No one wakes up in the morning and thinks first of all about how to screw up your day.

True peace comes from accepting your own anger, greed, and ignorance and turning them into tools for growing love.

This is hard. It's time to start.

🌿 🌿 🌿

WE HAVE MET THE ENEMY. POGO SAID THAT. YOU KNOW THE REST.

November 15

A mindful day.

This is a day of mindfulness. What is sought here is not a unique day, standing distinctly apart from all others, but a day when the practice of mindfulness moves into the foreground. Today is a day of enrichment and heightened awareness. Please bring this wonderful practice into every day.

Mindfulness is not an esoteric practice. Being mindful simply means being awake. For men, being mindful can mean the beginning of the end of the social masculine trance and the dismembered life. In mindfulness we become aware of the fullness and flow of our lives, one moment at a time.

The Appendix of this book contains specific directions and suggestions. I encourage you to visit a library or bookstore for additional help in this ancient practice. One excellent book is *Full Catastrophe Living* by Jon Kabat-Zinn, Ph.D. The Vietnamese Buddhist monk Thich Naht Hahn has written dozens of books, many of which concern mindfulness. My personal favorites are *The Miracle of Mindfulness* and *Being Peace*.

This is a beautiful day. Please embrace it fully.

November 16

*The woman who doesn't want to make a home
is undermining our nation.*
—Mrs. Thomas Alva Edison (1930)

This statement is laughable today, the sure target of sneers and high-camp humor.

Look closer. Suppose for a moment that this is true and that it became law? How would your life change? How is the nation weak and in what way would it be strengthened?

Look closer yet. Is the woman who does want to make a home the woman for you, really? Is that all she would do?

Does this statement make you feel a need to defend someone—your wife, perhaps, or someone else's?

In the years since Mrs. Edison said this, what's changed?

🌿 🌿 🌿

What's the same?

November 17

Where will you be when your laxative starts to work?
—Laxative ad

If we could see the future, our lives would not have been nearly as interesting as they have been thus far. But wouldn't it be nice if people weren't paid to write this stuff? If writing laxative copy or any ad copy at all was only a hobby, not through legislation but through, say, moral sensitivity, what might become of our time, our money, our imaginations?

Can you justify this advertisement?

Why would you bother?

※ ※ ※

WHERE WILL YOU BE WHEN SOMEONE ELSE'S LAXATIVE STARTS TO WORK?

November 18

Early to rise and early to bed,
makes a male healthy, wealthy and dead.
—JAMES THURBER

Where does the pressure come from, really, to pull ourselves out of bed each morning, effectively slamming the door on an important one third of our lives, shattering the remnants of dreams and leaving the sweet pressure of sheets and blankets without a moment of gratitude or regret? In monastic societies and in most lay religious practices, it is traditional to rise before dawn in order to pray, meditate, and greet the light. In these cases, early to rise and early to bed is motivated by the desire to honor the rhythms of the day and to be in touch with internal mental and spiritual processes.

Each day offers unique gifts and opportunities. The time spent in moving from waking to sleeping can be the time to integrate what is ceasing with what is beginning. What dream gifts were given in sleep? What unresolved discontent lingers to disturb the night?

Howard Thurman counseled Sam Keen never to get up on awaking and never to go to sleep on retiring, but to "simmer." Men who do only for others would be well served by a good long simmer twice a day and those who do only for themselves would benefit all the more.

WHAT'S THE HURRY?

November 19

The only sanity is Right Now!
—PAT RILEY

The daily practice of meditation is no longer solely the province of the mystic and the monk. Men worldwide have begun to spend alone-time each day to deepen the experience of the present moment. The regular practice of meditation, formally seated on a black cushion or simply alone in a private space "simmering," is enabling men to be more fully present throughout the course of the day. These men are discovering how little time they had spent in reality (sane that is), and how much of their lives had been spent in the illusory past or future.

Some men's groups begin their regular meetings with a few moments of silence and centering. The leader of the Convent Men's Group rings a bell three times at the beginning of each meeting and twice at the end to provide a reminder to be as fully conscious as possible of each moment between the soundings of the bell.

There are many books on meditation and there are teachers in most communities. I began by washing the dishes each night, mind focused only on the washing of the dishes. It is difficult, but "persistence furthers."

SANITY IS NOT THE RESULT OF MEDITATION, IT IS THE REALITY OF IT.

November 20

I know that my home can be many things. Is it the place for my ego or my soul?

<small>WHAT DOES HOME MEAN TO YOU? WRITE ABOUT IT.</small>

November 21

. . . if we do not change our daily lives, we cannot change the world.
—THICH NHAT HANH

We have been driven by a thousand unsatisfied needs and have been manipulated by manifold thousand needs and chronic discontents of others. We said that this is the way of the world and went ahead with tolerating it, all the while destroying our lives and our habitat by our simple inability to notice where we were and what we were doing.

It is different for men today. We are awakening to the simple realities of the details of our ordinary lives.

David Spangler points out that a trip to the supermarket is an occasion for mindfulness. When we acknowledge all the hands that brought us the food, we become conscious of its true cost and its great value. Working consciously, mindful of the great net of people and material that participates in this work, teaches us what it is we are really doing.

Although grocery shopping and work are only two examples of activities we can perform mindfully, we are empowered to change the world by deepening our appreciation of them. When we see how food comes to us, perhaps we will change our eating habits. When we see some results of our work, perhaps we will reconsider its value.

TODAY I WILL LOOK DEEPLY AT MY CONSUMING
AND MY PRODUCING.

November 22

We really need each other in spiritual life just as we do in our more ordinary pursuits.
—FRANCES VAUGHAN

The spiritual life is personal but not secret. As men, we have bought the myth of self-reliance and, if we had a conscious spiritual life at all, we would usually share only our convictions and rarely our doubts. Our spiritual honor was unquestionable—and unquestioned.

The past few decades have been a time of questioning, relentless and demanding. The sound of thunder told of the coming storm. We learned to sit together in the shelter of community in order to hear the greater teachings of wonder and awe. The teachings were familiar ones to all of us. They told us that we were not alone and that we could only grow codependently. Our fears were held in common. We felt such release when the guys told us that they too were sleepless over money-fear, sex-fear, and power-fear. We were comforted to learn that we were not alone in our rage and impotence. We felt the union of men reaching for simple harmony.

We stand naked with our partners. Our children hear us acknowledge our frailty and see our strength in not turning aside from it.

GOD SITS NEXT TO US ON THE BUS, READING THE PAPER AND
WORRYING ABOUT HER WORLD.

November 23

Men have been wild with grief for too long. We have been narcotized, compartmentalized, and dismembered. Along the way we have cut pieces out of our hearts and sliced up our bodies for someone else's banquet.

The healing began, in Burroughs's words, at that "... frozen moment when everyone sees what is on the end of every fork."

The awakening comes when we take responsibility, without equivocation and without blame, for what has happened in us. Our grief has served us well. Our rage finally broke our hearts. We could voice our feelings of uselessness. We took our balls and went home. Game's over and everybody's out.

🌳 🌳 🌳

IS THERE ANYONE LEFT TO BLAME?

November 24

*What was it missing, then, at the man's heart
so that he does not wound?*
—JOHN BERRYMAN

That wondrous male heart was whole and complete, needing nothing in itself; it lacked only an entryway. It beat on behind a carapace of hostility and sorrow. We called our hearts "hard" when they were only hidden.

What finally broke was not the heart but the rough crust.

Tender-hearted men have always been with us, a small tribe of impassioned guys who are the new models, razing the myth of the warrior and expelling the toxic masculine.

🌳 🌳 🌳

WHOM WOULD YOU PUT ON THE LIST? MINE INCLUDES STEWART UDALL, JAMES PARK MORTON, AND ROBERT BLY.

November 25

We are a divided species—head running ahead of heart. It is no surprise that coronary thrombosis is the characteristic death of our time. The heart literally chokes up on the impossibility of keeping up.
—BRIAN ALDISS

Men die of heart disease at a rate far greater than that for women. This is not a metaphor for anything; it is the awful reality of a culture gone mad to consume until it finally consumes itself, with men as the identified producers.

We are starting to suspect that there is a secret shame about this role. Work is not what is killing us. Coping with our work and our lives is what is busting the arteries. We got overweight, underexercised, addicted to food, alcohol, drugs, and pure speed just to get along with our work and our shame.

Now men are asking themselves if the prize is overvalued. Annihilation of body or spirit is a high price to pay for money, sex, and power.

WHAT'S WORTH DYING FOR?

November 26

When I feel driven to be entertained, I will look at the addiction rather than the stage.

Make a list of your favorite movies. What do the men in them have in common?

November 27

Dancing is a very crude attempt to get into the rhythm of life.
—GEORGE BERNARD SHAW

Never stop dancing.

It's undignified, juvenile, embarrassing, strenuous, and unmanly. A man must be responsible and serious and dancing just doesn't fit in—except for the box step at some family member's wedding. In a suit and tie.

Dancing is the full body equivalent of growl growing to shout collapsing to brainless laughter. It is a difficult exercise when body and mind are disconnected. Maybe neckties are at fault. Look at Richard Nixon—not dancing, of course, but simply trying to walk on the beach. He couldn't do it without conscious effort, and his idea of playing with a yo-yo was to make sure it went all the way to the end of the string and stayed.

We severed our dancing legs on the way to the top. Maybe we can find them on the joyous trip back down.

🌳 🌳 🌳

NEVER STOP DANCING.

November 28

To every thing there is a season, and a time to every purpose under the heaven....
—ECCLESIASTES 3:1

There is no one way to be a man anymore than there is one way to be water. A man's life does not unfold outside of time or space but in them. If, at fifty, I was the same person I was at twenty, I would either be miserable or thirty years in the grave. If, at fifty, I think that a man of twenty should be like me, I have wasted the experience of the thirty years that separate me from him.

My life as a man is mine alone, lived in my seasons and in the places I have been, and it is unique for that fact, but it is also driven by the same forces that drive us all and, in that, is nothing special. I owe my fellows the stories that grow from my experience, without the demand that they repeat those stories. I owe myself and them the reality of their seasons and places.

WHOSE STORY AM I LIVING?

November 29

No more man is more cheated than the selfish man.
—HENRY WARD BEECHER

Our selfishness isolates us from our fellows. It can be manifested in many ways, some grotesque and obvious ("I don't see what's in it for me"), some subtle ("I'm doing it all for the kids"), and some in hellish disguise ("The American people want . . .").

We can be materially selfish, getting all the toys before we die; emotionally selfish, demanding love, respect, and power, unshared and undeserved; and spiritually selfish, the prayer "my will, not thine, be done" rolling out of the mind while the mouth speaks other words.

THE WAY OUT OF SELFISHNESS AND THE WAY OUT OF ISOLATION ARE THE SAME—HARD WORK AND SELF-AWARENESS. AND JUST A LITTLE BIT OF JOY.

I know that recollection of the details of my past enlivens the present.

DESCRIBE YOUR MOTHER AS YOU SAW HER
WHEN YOU WERE A CHILD.

December 1

This is a month of spiritual preparation, dedication, and enlightenment. It is the Advent Season, a time of preparation for the coming of the light. It is the time of the eight-day festival of lights set at the dark of the moon, called Hanukkah. In the Zen Buddhist tradition, this is the time of Rohatsu, or Bodhi Day, the celebration of the Buddha's enlightenment and the enlightenment of all beings, and it is the time for the Taoist festival of reflection and renewal, Ta Chin.

We can take time out from the busyness of holiday preparation to consider our spirits. What is our relationship to Earth, Heart, and Hearth? Perhaps we can make this a month of deeper devotion to those three, and of deeper awareness of the place they occupy in our lives. One possibility for devotion and awareness is to initiate or increase attendance at communal gatherings such as men's groups, church, or temple. Another is to prepare a garden for spring by planting bulbs or building a compost pile.

The most fertile method, perhaps, is to simply throw oneself into the season with total abandon. We can dare to hold nothing back and to be guided by the spirit.

December 2

Besides the noble art of getting things done, there is the noble art of leaving things undone. The wisdom of life consists in the elimination of nonessentials.
—LIN YUTANG

The busy, busy man, doing, fixing, and looking ahead for more to do and fix, is not too different from a cat overdosed on laxatives—crapping, covering up, and looking for new places to crap.

We have harmed ourselves ourselves greatly by not cultivating the art of not-doing. First, we lost the gift of the quiet mind, open to intuition and insight. We forced our wills and our reason into every situation and lost our creativity along the way. We need to relearn the wisdom of the old cliché that says "don't just do something, sit there."

We have also harmed by failing to let those we love learn their own lessons. Motivated by fear, we tried to protect our children and ended up leaving them weak and without simple skills that can be learned only from experience. We were afraid our lovers would be hurt by some circumstance, so we betrayed them with our ego-driven controlling, leaving them defenseless when alone.

WE NEED TO LEARN THE DIFFERENCE BETWEEN THE BUSINESS OF LIVING AND THE BUSYNESS.

December 3

Age is only a cipher, a number for the records. A man can't retire his experience. He must use it.
—Bernard M. Baruch

Our culture puts many unreasonable demands upon its men, but none of them is more dishonorable than the one which says, "You're old and undesirable. You no longer have useful muscles and your ideas are old-fashioned. Please sit in the sun, quietly." In a simple and tender society, we would bow to our elders and ask for their teachings. We would not be repelled by their age, but in awe of it. We would not ask that they become clowns or kings but that they sit down with us and tell us their stories.

It is the old man who knows to ask a child about the desires of her heart and to remind her father to do the same. The old man sitting in his lawn chair in old cop clothes, waving to the drivers who wave to him, brings more joy and teachings in his madness than any dour and rational businessman nodding from his isolation, rushing to work.

We honor our elders as we honor our children:
by listening to them with open hearts.

December 4

This is war:
Boys flung into a breach
like shoveled earth;
and old men,
Broken
Driving rapidly before crowds of people
In a glitter of silly decorations.
Behind the boys
And the old men
Life weeps
And sheds her garments
To the blowing winds.
—AMY LOWELL

The tender-hearted man, experienced and open, refuses war by refusing to be warlike. He will not sacrifice boys because he has learned that the boy in him is not hateful. He is fierce in his determination that on his watch, no child will die; nor will he permit children to die to save children from dying.

He is not a popular man with some, but his tribe is growing because so many men have begun to question the warrior myth, the manly myth, and are saying that its time is past. They serve peace by being peaceful. They are connected with each other. They learn from each other and they turn to the female for her teachings.

THIS MAN NURTURES PEACE IN HIMSELF, DAILY.

December 5

There is darkness; it is the companion of light.

In winter, the earth fuses and the light is short. Nothing is growing in sight. Only Elsinore is visible, just over the horizon.

Now is the time of surrender to the insistence of life. Plants are blooming underground to be forced through the cracked surface when the light returns. Now too we can surrender to the knowledge of betrayal and guilt, which is often not seen in bright sun and sparkling air. We can enter the dark castle with faith that healing grows in the dark, waiting for the sun.

The journey into darkness is mandatory and it is taken alone. However, we can follow the threads left by the ancestors, in myth or in family stories. Our fathers and our mentors have taken this journey. Some have returned. If we ask, they will point the way.

I CAN ALSO ENTER THE DARKNESS BY OFFERING MY HAND TO THOSE WHO SUFFER.

December 6

A mindful day.

This is a day of mindfulness. What is sought here is not a unique day, standing distinctly apart from all others, but a day when the practice of mindfulness moves into the foreground. Today is a day of enrichment and heightened awareness. Please bring this wonderful practice into every day.

Mindfulness is not an esoteric practice. Being mindful simply means being awake. For men, being mindful can mean the beginning of the end of the social masculine trance and the dismembered life. In mindfulness we become aware of the fullness and flow of our lives, one moment at a time.

The Appendix of this book contains specific directions and suggestions. I encourage you to visit a library or bookstore for additional help in this ancient practice. One excellent book is *Full Catastrophe Living* by Jon Kabat-Zinn, Ph.D. The Vietnamese Buddhist monk Thich Naht Hahn has written dozens of books, many of which concern mindfulness. My personal favorites are *The Miracle of Mindfulness* and *Being Peace*.

This is a beautiful day. Please embrace it fully.

December 7

We shall not cease from exploration
And the end of all our exploring
Will be to arrive where we started
And know the place for the first time.
—T.S. ELIOT

Eventually every one of us will come to the point in our lives where there is only one barrier left. We will have passed by or failed at the others by now, or perhaps we skipped some of them entirely.

The final exam is mandatory. We can't cram.

Shunryu Suzuki suggests that each of us find another way to speak of dying and see how it changes our living. What would that word be?

A MAN WHO HAS LEARNED LIVING AND TAUGHT IT, IN HIS LIVING
AND IN HIS STORIES, HAS A FINAL OBLIGATION.
HE MUST TEACH HOW TO DIE.

December 8

Hope and Fear cannot alter the seasons.
—CHOGYAM TRUNGPA
Rinpoche

When we can see our lives as an unfolding series of gifts that we cannot control, rather than as a challenge to be met or a game to be played, with money, sex, and power as the markers, we banish hope and fear.

Living without fear is clearly desirable, but what joy can be found in a life without hope? T.S. Eliot counsels to "wait without hope/ for it would be hope for the wrong thing." We limit our futures if we alone decide what that future holds. Our limited hopes are really desires dressed up in vaguely spiritual garments. We say, "I hope that thus and so will come to me," but we often mean that we need or demand that outcome.

So "hope" generates fear and fear generates more desire, which generates more addiction, and we are left in the mire of either needs that have not been met or, often worse, needs that *have* been met and are seen, too late, as petty and selfish. The spirit suffers and the soul is wounded.

DO I HAVE EVERYTHING I NEED? DO I HAVE EVERYTHING I WANT?

December 9

But too many people now climb onto the cross merely to be seen from a greater distance, even if they have to trample somewhat on the one who has been there so long.
—ALBERT CAMUS

We have not been crucified because of our gender. Many men have been victimized, but not because they are men. Many people have been victimized by the corrupting pressures of a materialistic society and by the outmoded patriarchy, men among them. We are not alone.

Some say that men were the last to get the message. We need to hear in that message a call to action rather than to martyrdom. The masculine spirit seeks to join rather than to separate. There are great problems to be faced, knots to be untied, and walls to be dismantled.

The man who insists on his continued separation, whether in his "den" or on the cross, is part of the problem.

🌿 🌿 🌿

WHEN I BEGIN TO PLAY MARTYR, I WILL SILENTLY TELL MYSELF TO GROW UP.

December 10

In our rich consumers' society we spin cocoons around ourselves and get possessed by our possessions.
—MAX LERNER

As men work to develop a new male consciousness, they are learning, to their dismay, that the patterns of consuming and producing to consume have been at the base of much of their discontent. They are discovering that they were sold an empty box by the boardwalk hustler who now shows up on envelopes promising million-dollar prizes. (What could be more satisfying than knowing "you have already won . . ."?) It is as if the dreams of security and property were drug-induced euphorias with no grounding in the reality of self and place.

The spiritual life that is now opening to men is a rich one. We are seeking to serve rather than being served. We are developing a natural perspective, based on experience, contemplation, and attentiveness. Concurrently we are accepting that the material life is not a "bad" life anymore than alcohol is a "bad" drug—the problem is in the man, not in the life or the drug.

THE COCOON FALLS AWAY. OUR VISION SHIFTS. WE OWN OUR LIVES WHEN OUR POSSESSIONS NO LONGER POSSESS US.

December 11

Life makes numerous demands on a man. At many points along the way we need to go contrary to the force of our instincts and desires in order to serve a larger good. Our dignity would be lost in failing to be counterinstinctual. The "natural man" is about seven years old. The instincts, left untamed, would destroy us while leaving us standing in place. It is in the perversion of these instincts, for security, companionship, and a place in the natural order, that we may lose our dignity and our spirit.

However, we also see that the counterinstinctual life, secretly ego-driven, the life of conspicuous virtue and self-denial, has bled many more men of their true power than has the life of blind satisfaction of the basic instincts.

In looking to the needs of the soul, a man finds the balance between these two poles. The soul recoils as quickly from the popinjay as from the pedagogue.

THE DAILY PRACTICE OF MINDFULNESS AND HONESTY IN THE PURSUIT OF A USEFUL LIFE IS THE PRACTICE OF THE SPIRITED MAN.

December 12

To say yes, you have to sweat and roll up your sleeves and plunge both hands into life up to the elbows. It is easy to say no, even if saying no means death.
—JEAN ANOUILH

We've said no in countless ways, but often our noes have been disguised as yesses. We have said yes to the myths of our families and our culture without question and have said no in the process to a fuller appreciation of the riches both have to offer. These ersatz yesses have produced generations of soft men, make-believe warriors, and endless boyhoods.

Now we are putting an end to this foolishness. Each day we are uncovering our lives and spirits. Each day that we spend in mindful attention to what is about us and care lovingly for whatever that is for us, we are claiming it as our own. We are practicing love and that, we are finding, requires sweat and harder work than any we have done thus far.

WE ARE IN OUR LIVES "UP TO THE ELBOWS" AND SAYING YES, FIERCELY AND JOYFULLY. THE INVOLVED MAN REJOICES IN THE VIGOR OF HIS AWAKENING.

December 13

Do not seek to follow in the footsteps of the men of old:
seek what they sought.
—Matsuo Basho

The path is fresh in spite of every foot that has touched it. As we move away from the wonderful pursuits of boyhood and seek to find some of the man-rhythm to dance to, we are going to a familiar place by a route that can only be uniquely our own. I cannot go the way my teachers have gone, although I am going where they too are headed. If I follow Sam's route or if Travis follows mine, we're missing the experience of the trip.

WHOSE DESTINATION IS AHEAD?

December 14

It is our duty to compose our character, not to compose books, and to win, not battles and provinces, but order and tranquility for our conduct of life.
—MONTAIGNE

As our perspective has changed and we have been able to place the spiritual ahead of the material and intimacy above isolation, we are discovering gifts of serenity and purposefulness that we could not previously have imagined. We do not need to change what we do, in most cases, because we have changed how and why we do what we do. Many men, in awakening to the spirited masculine, have remained outwardly much the same. The change is an inward one and as we work for that change and, daily, openly acknowledge the fruits of that work, we sense the possibility of halting the escalation of corruption and war all around us.

When we cease to pollute ourselves, we begin to end the pollution of our greater environment. As we seek to "compose our character" we create harmony rather than disorder.

WHEN WE SEEK SERENITY, WE WIN PEACE.

December 15

Transformation is the word. We can do the work of
transformation only in the present moment.
—THICH NHAT HANH

Overcoming destructive social conditioning and remembering our lives is the beginning of a man's journey,
not the end. All the preliminary work was basically a matter of setting up the pins. Our true task is to join with the
world so completely that who we were is forgotten and
what we are becoming is not an issue. Peace exists in
wholeness, and wholeness is found only in this moment,
right here. Transformation would not be possible without
all that has gone before, but it is impossible if we dwell on
the path behind us. We hope that all the talk of a "men's
movement" will fade in time and that we will join with the
feminine and be transformed. The divisiveness born of the
masculine spiritual awakening was inevitable; its perpetua-
tion must be unacceptable.

IN DOING THE WORK RIGHT IN FRONT OF US, MINDFULLY AND
LOVINGLY, WE ARE TRANSFORMED. IN SIMPLY LIVING TODAY,
WE ARE ENLIGHTENED.

December 16

It is a rare life that remains well ordered even in private. Any man can play his part in the side show and represent a worthy man on the boards. . . .
—MONTAIGNE

Hell is probably neat, well scheduled, and in perfect order. The flames burn at a uniform and unimaginable heat and the demons' uniforms are laundered daily. Each tormented soul knows what is coming next, always.

We have so ordered our external lives, with scheduled work, obsessive play, and endless entertainment, that we are without quiet and are, by determined effort, deaf to the questions of the spirit. Yet, for all the appearance of order, chaos rules our inner lives. We have only increased the inner madness in our attempts to control or ignore it.

By shifting our attention to the present moment rather than keeping it upon any amusement or busyness that will distract us from it, we discover, to our surprise, a great peace and a great power.

This morning, the early sun in my office fell on my little boy's face in such a way that his eyelashes were vividly highlighted. I was, for a moment, lost in his profile. When he left, with the pencil he needed, I returned to my work and found it so much easier than it had been when it occupied my nearest horizon.

SIMPLE BREATHING AND AWARENESS OF WHAT IS BEFORE US CREATES AN ORDER THAT ALL THE COMPULSIVE BUSYNESS WE ARE ACCUSTOMED TO CAN NEVER APPROXIMATE.

December 17

You may not call me naive. If you must label me, you may call me "not cynical."
—MOLLY BRODSKY

We tell ourselves that we are being "realistic" when what we are doing is running away from reality. We submerge our feelings by being worldly while our world lies in ruin. Our cynicism, our hyper-busyness, and our compulsion to be endlessly entertained have often served to suppress the awful reality of the slow death of the earth, the "poverty of affluence," and the end of full-tilt, deeply engaged living.

Tender-hearted men are seen as naive. We are not—not if naive implies passivity and ineffectiveness. But we are—if by naive we mean questioning, innocent, and willing to risk embarrassment or failure.

❦ ❦ ❦

WHEN THE MAN TELLS ME "HOW IT IS,"
I'LL TURN TO THE BOY.

December 18

When I find myself only thinking about the suffering of others, I will mindfully turn to action.

COOK AN EXTRA PORTION OF DINNER AND SET A PLACE AT YOUR TABLE TO ACKNOWLEDGE THOSE WITHOUT FOOD AND HOMES.

December 19

When I become blasé about the gifts I have been given, I will take action to revive those blessings.

THANK A MAN WHO HAS INSPIRED OR MENTORED YOU THIS YEAR FOR DOING SO. BE SPECIFIC. TAKE PLENTY OF TIME.

When I become blasé about the gifts I have been given, I will take action to revive those blessings.

THANK A WOMAN WHO HAS INSPIRED OR MENTORED YOU THIS
YEAR FOR DOING SO. BE SPECIFIC. TAKE PLENTY OF TIME.

December 21

When I become blasé about the gifts I have been given, I will take action to revive those blessings.

🌳 🌳 🌳

THANK A CHILD WHO HAS INSPIRED OR MENTORED YOU THIS YEAR FOR DOING SO. BE SPECIFIC. TAKE PLENTY OF TIME.

December 22

Look more deeply at this popular slogan.

Much of our suffering comes from the assumption that we should always feel good: that when the mean nasties come along, the surly supervisor, the long line at the bank, the neighbors' affection for The Osmonds, played loud, or the children's refusal to be grateful for our hard work, we have a god-given right not to have to feel crumby. We do not have that right. In addition, we do not, as the slogan above might imply, have the privilege of not suffering. Life is loaded with suffering. The problem has been that we refused to feel it. We stuffed ourselves with substances or surrounded ourselves with things or busied ourselves with yearning and earning, all not to suffer, not to be fully alive.

Suffering is not optional. Suffering is human. Our option with suffering is to let it *be*.

I CAN LOOK MORE DEEPLY AT SLOGANS, CLICHES, OR ASSUMPTIONS
THAT SOUND RIGHT ONLY BECAUSE THEY SOUND GOOD.

December 23

I find nothing in fables more astonishing than my experience in every hour. One moment of a man's life is a fact so stupendous as to take the lustre out of all fiction.
—RALPH WALDO EMERSON

As we practice mindful living, living awake and noticing the moments of our lives as they happen rather than before or after they happen, we heal the years of wounding with moments of wonder. It is not easy to break the habits of years of sleepwalking. In this book, there are only twelve days in the year devoted specifically to mindfulness, but for many of us those will be twelve days such as we have not experienced previously.

There is great pressure on men to miss the appointment we have made with life in order to keep the appointments we make with illusion, often appointments we didn't make ourselves. We are breaking those appointments now, forced meetings with the judges of our proper performance, and keeping the appointment with the full spectrum of every small moment. When we are walking in the park, we are fully there rather than tasting over and over the bitter aftertaste of a spat with our partners, rather than having a conversation with a co-worker about the press of deadlines.

I CAN PRACTICE STAYING PLANTED TODAY.

December 24

Are modern folk, perhaps, afraid of night? Do they fear the vast serenity, the mystery of infinite space, the austerity of stars?
—HENRY BESTON

There is a canyon deep in the Los Padres National Forest in Big Sur, California, where the nights are as black as any I've seen. I've been there in all seasons, nearly always alone, usually for three or four days at a time. It is as dark as the mind of Satan there, after the last sunlight fades from the canyon walls.

On one trip I made, two couples came gallumping down the trail in their new boots, just at dusk. They set up marvelous tents, cooked meat, drank whiskey, and listened to a battery powered radio, laughing and talking deep into the early morning, lanterns hissing.

I was glad they were there. That was the first trip I made in which I hadn't drunk brandy all day to keep away the night. I was afraid of the dark then. I had lost the sense of awe I knew as a child, at night, in Tennessee fields far from the light of the farmhouse. I had become an adult without becoming a man. Solitude and the dark held mind-beasts I could not confront. That was fifteen years ago. I long to go back to the Little Sur River and celebrate the thick dark.

THE CHILD AND THE SPIRITED MAN WALK IN THE BEAUTY OF THE NIGHT.

December 25

Write a prayer of awakening.

December 26

A mindful day.

This is a day of mindfulness. What is sought here is not a unique day, standing distinctly apart from all others, but a day when the practice of mindfulness moves into the foreground. Today is a day of enrichment and heightened awareness. Please bring this wonderful practice into every day.

Mindfulness is not an esoteric practice. Being mindful simply means being awake. For men, being mindful can mean the beginning of the end of the social masculine trance and the dismembered life. In mindfulness we become aware of the fullness and flow of our lives, one moment at a time.

The Appendix of this book contains specific directions and suggestions. I encourage you to visit a library or bookstore for additional help in this ancient practice. One excellent book is *Full Catastrophe Living* by Jon Kabat-Zinn, Ph.D. The Vietnamese Buddhist monk Thich Naht Hahn has written dozens of books, many of which concern mindfulness. My personal favorites are *The Miracle of Mindfulness* and *Being Peace*.

This is a beautiful day. Please embrace it fully.

December 27

*. . . I don't have to collect spiritual knowledge. If it fits, it'll find
a place in my heart, like music fits into your ear.*
—ARLO GUTHRIE

It's too easy to fall into the trap of spiritual materialism. It's been said that there are as many emotional fascists
dressed in the spiritual uniform, all-white or monk's robes,
as in the military one. There are designer humility clothes
for the seeker just as there are designer farmer clothes for
the suburban fop in his Jeep Wrangler. Our intellects can
become as crammed as our closets with the stuff of the
stuff-free life. The dilemma of materialism is always with
us. We are not going to unlearn instantly the habits of accumulation that we have spent years perfecting.

It is for just this reason that we are beginning to learn
the practice of mindfulness. When we see clearly what we
are doing and can smile at our foolishness, our foolishness
can end.

THE COSTUME AND LIBRARY OF THE HOLY MAN DON'T FIT TOO
WELL IN MOST MEN'S HOMES.

December 28

When a man is in the leader position, whether later in his life out of his sheer experience or as a father of children, wherever he finds them, he is obligated to be candid and open about his missteps along the way. We have had enough of lying and cover-ups to last several generations in our public and private lives. We're not going to leave the false trails, as tempting and as easy as it might be. We tell those who depend on our teachings what the false teachings are. We don't say "don't go this way," but we do say "there are some terrible prices to pay for not much gain down this road. There be tigers."

Mr. Gravy tells kids at his camp that he used to brush his teeth with a Snickers bar and when they laugh (the kids, not his teeth), he takes out his bridge and shows them the stumps of his teenaged teeth. "Brush 'em if you got 'em," he hollers.

WE EARNED OUR SCARS AND STUMPS AND
WE MUST SHARE THEIR STORIES.

December 29

In the safety of that community (the Church) I can discuss spiritual and ethical issues freely, giving voice to feelings and beliefs kept too long in the shadows.
—LYNN WILLEFORD

The places to feel the presence of God have always been nearby. We have passed the Church of the Temple on the way to work, school, or the entertainment palaces. We passed them without much notice, and often with some secret guilt at having left them many years before. Even those who continued to go to these places felt the anxiety of having abandoned them in their hearts.

The spiritual ache would not go away, no matter how hard we tried to ignore it. We were embarrassed at hearing words like *spiritual*, *God*, *worship*, and the like. But we listened more closely to those conversations, feigning disinterest or indulgence of those clearly weaker than ourselves.

Finally, we could no longer ignore the urgency we felt to embrace the spiritual once more. When men begin to return to the spiritual life, often with the help of other men and often after repeated failures to find true comfort in some material pursuit, they return with open hearts and deep curiosity about their own greater selves. They are not church-goers so much as life-goers who have found a place of kindred spirits.

❦ ❦ ❦

WHERE IS MY CHURCH? WHO GOES THERE?

December 30

Integration of [the] new self into one's life and family and society is the greatest and most difficult challenge in spiritual practice.
—STEPHEN MITCHELL

When men first became aware of their dissatisfaction with the status quo and realized that the material rewards of money and power and the adoring glances of the women were miserable compensation for the dismemberment they had suffered, and when they said "enough of this," they were not greeted with much love by those they challenged. The first leaders of the "men's movement" were mocked or criticized by most, and most often by other men. Those who came later entered an arena made unpopular by the popular culture. But we came anyway. The spiritual pain was too great to be ignored just because we were no longer "being good." We turned our backs on Woman, put aside what we thought we were supposed to be, for a while, and looked into our hearts to find the teachings there.

We found that when our community cannot understand what we have learned, then we must be teachers. We must also understand that those who have always known us will probably insist on seeing who we were rather than who we have become. The family needs stasis, no matter what the cost. Our teaching will go unheard there but our living will be noticed.

THE REALITY IS THIS: DO AS I DO, NOT AS I SAY.

December 31

Waking up in the morning
I vow with all beings
to be ready for sparks of the Dharma
from flowers or children or birds.
—ROBERT AITKEN, *Roshi*

At the end of the year, we must vow renewal one day at a time. This contemporary Buddhist *gatha*, a short verse to be recited to bring one to mindfulness, is offered for use in daily renewal.

Here is a Christian prayer to accompany it. Please use them well.

My Lord God, I have no idea where I am going. I do not see the road ahead of me. I cannot know for certain where it will end. Nor do I really know myself, and the fact that I think I am following your will does not mean that I am actually doing so. But I believe that the desire to please you does in fact please you. And I hope that I have that desire in all that I am doing. I hope that I will never do anything apart from that desire. And I know that if I do this you will lead me by the right road, though I may know nothing about it. Therefore I will trust you always though I may seem lost and in the shadow of death. I will not fear, for you are ever with me, and you will never leave me to face my perils alone.
—THOMAS MERTON

Appendix
Suggestions for a Mindful Day

A mindful day.

This day is intended to deepen our appreciation of the present moment and to be energized by it. It is a difficult practice in our ordinary lives, usually reserved for "days off" or, more commonly, monastic life. Here, it is secularized and made gentle. It may appear difficult. It is not; it is merely different. Please take some time to accustom yourself to these exercises. They need not be done perfectly and, on some days, some may prove impossible. If that is the case, it is useful to see why they seem to be undoable. That alone is being mindful. Here are the suggestions. Practice as many as possible. In time you should be able to increase the number and frequency.

Just Say No

Do not consume today. Buy nothing that is not essential to your survival. Stay away from catalogues and store windows.

No "fast" food. If possible, prepare your own meals today. Refrain from frivolous conversation. Take Robert Bly's advice and yell a Haiku when you're caught in a boring conversation.

Do not read the newspapers today; do without television today; do not be "entertained" today.

Conscious Breathing

The core exercise for mindfulness is conscious breathing. Whenever you are missing your appointment with life; when you are angry and distressed or rushing about; when you want to "get control" of some person, place, or thing—these are some of the times to detach and watch your breath. Breathe in and out, slowly and long. Think to yourself, "breathing in, I know I am breathing in. Breathing out, I know I am breathing out". Repeat this for as long as you can. Try to notice only your breath during these periods. On this day, make an agreement with yourself to watch your breath. For example, you can agree to take five minutes of each hour, wherever you are, to breathe consciously.

Hang Time in a Sacred Place

Twice today, for about thirty minutes in the morning and evening, find a quiet and private place, your sacred place, where you will not be disturbed. Use it selfishly. Quiet your mind with breathing. You can light incense and then listen to a favorite piece of music, if possible, or reread a favorite poem. Perhaps you have a picture of yourself as a child or of some ancestor. Have a loving conversation with that person. If you keep a diary or would like to begin that practice, this is the time to write in it. Try to avoid thinking about your work or family worries. When such thoughts arise, notice them, without judgment, and turn resolutely to your "selfishness." This is a special time for your soul and spirit. With practice you will learn how best to use it. Daily practice of Hang Time is a vitalizing experience.

Perhaps this is the time for that meditation practice you always meant to begin. There are many excellent books on meditation in the library or bookstores. You could use this day to find one that appeals to you.

Where Am I?

This exercise can be practiced many times during the day. Make an agreement with yourself to practice it at certain times, for example when you are on the bus or sitting in a meeting. There are many opportunities.

To locate yourself, first breathe in and out consciously for a moment or so. Then move your consciousness through your body randomly. Ask yourself, for example, "Where are my feet?" You might answer, "My feet are cocked back under my chair. My right foot is at an outward angle. My left foot is pointed straight ahead." Throughout this locating, continue to breathe fully. You can locate your buttocks, your ears, your hands, your knees. Generally, the mind will be directed to those parts of your body that are "elsewhere." After locating your body, ask yourself the purpose of its location. "I am here, in this posture on the train going to work."

Slow Walking

When you are on the move today, slow down. Consciously walk slowly, matching your breath to your steps. Take a few steps, slowly, and count the number of steps you take while inhaling and while exhaling. Then, as you walk, count these same numbers of steps with every complete breath. Notice the feel of the earth or floor beneath your feet. Allow yourself to feel the connection, without judgment. Walk like this for just a few minutes several times today. Notice how alive you feel. When your mind wanders to the next meeting, to your home, to regrets, or worries, notice this, without judgment and return to your Slow Walking. If possible, find some uncrowded place like a park or your backyard and walk like this for a longer period. Could this, too, become a daily practice?

A Full Meal

Choose one meal to prepare entirely by yourself. If you are not used to cooking, this is the time to learn. Keep it simple and pay attention to every moment. Use fresh foods, unprocessed, unprepared and wholesome. This might be a good time to make an entirely vegetarian meal.

The important thing is this: Be aware of every step in the process of preparing this meal. When you shop, notice the colors and textures of foods. Notice how many people work in the market to bring this food to you. Are there delivery trucks? Are they local, or is this food from outside of your region? As you chop the vegetables, endeavor to do nothing else. If your hands are chopping and your mind is in conversation with a colleague, you are missing supper. Take your time. Let your eyes rest on the food. Consider how many hands were involved in the preparation of this meal.

Perhaps you could offer a prayer of gratitude before beginning to eat. If you are eating with your family or with friends, try eating in silence. If this is too tall an order, eat silently for only the first ten minutes of the meal. Take time to look at your companions and smile.

When cleaning the dishes and the kitchen, breathe in and out consciously. Notice how much cleaner everything gets.

Lights Out

At bedtime, don't go to bed. You might want to take a long bath with candles, music, or incense first. Perhaps you could walk, slowly and mindfully, indoors or outdoors. If you have a favorite piece of music or book of poetry, this could be the time to listen or read. The important thing is to be alone, quiet, and in the present moment. This is not the time for dream-weaving.

When you go to bed, don't go to sleep. Howard

Thurman advised Sam Keen to "simmer" at bedtime. There is no better word. Simmer. What resentments are you carrying? Heal them by smiling. What conversation was unfinished? Finish it, lovingly. What else was left undone? Finish it if you can, or let it be, with a smile.

Breathing consciously, in and out, weave dreams.

BILL ALEXANDER is an editor, actor and writer. He is the founder of The Fathers' Group, a web of storytellers, artists, executives, and adventurers, who are actively involved in re-visioning fathers' tasks.

He and his family divide their time between Convent Station, New Jersey and Westport, New York.

Lind Elman
Ca
New york (-
C

212 - 975 - 4321

[> Cath Conroy
Eug man ris
♯ 10:30